I0579137

Praise for *Ely Air Lines*

The *Ely Air Lines* book series captures what's most important about general aviation flying—the people and the relationships. Through this compilation of newspaper columns, Mike Ely and Linda Street-Ely recount the stories about people and places uncovered as they travel by general aviation airplane, their Grumman Cheetah pulling the thread that stitches together the tales of the remarkable personalities they encounter.

Sometimes sad, sometimes humorous, always entertaining and thoughtful, each short story heralds the benefits of general aviation aircraft and airports. This is the sort of reporting that will make the masses care about general aviation and help us protect the freedom to fly.

—Mark Baker
President and CEO, AOPA

The *Ely Air Lines* books offer the reader an easy look into a wide variety of aviation activities and experiences. The 100 short stories included offer the option of break-time reading as well as serious rainy-weather diversion.

These stories are relevant for pilots to expand their aviation knowledge, and for non-pilots to gain a better insight into the strengths, passions, and quirks—basically, the humanity—of pilots. These stories provide an inside view of aviation missing from the daily sound-bite news. Definitely recommended reading.

—Richard VanGrunsven
Founder and CEO of Van's Aircraft Inc.

The *Ely Air Lines* books provide the reader a throwback to the better and easier days of more pleasure and fewer rules. Their short stories are an easy reminder of why we all fell in love with aviation.

Simply reading a few lines and I'm captured in a story, away from the daily hustle and bustle, that I enjoy and will learn from. An easy read that will relax the mind, and leave the reader wishing for their own blue sky adventures. Absolutely recommended reading.

– Nina Keefer
Co-founder and Chief Pilot of Anthelion Helicopters

Pure enjoyment is what one will experience while reading the stories from the Elys' book series. Not only does it bring back many memories, but it also gives an insight to the people and events that are the reason we are all so passionate about aviation.

– Debby Rihn-Harvey
U.S. National and World Aerobatic Champion, retired airline captain, FBO and flight school business owner, FAA Designated Pilot Examiner, mentor

What began with the passionate efforts of Linda Street-Ely and Mike Ely to promote their beloved community airport evolved into a delightful collection of perceptive commentaries from deep inside the grassroots of American aviation.

This two-volume collection of the Elys' column in their local Texas newspaper quietly opens up the fascinating world of life at little airports – and the lives of the people who frequent them. It has long been said that there are more characters per capita in aviation than any other human endeavor. It's true.

These books by Linda and Mike capture the quirks, the fascinating, and the sometimes selfless greatness of aviators who find joy in going aloft in flying machines—ranging from the most modest to snap-your-head-back monsters that snort and bellow their way over the horizon before you can blink.

Because they were newspaper columns, most stories are brief. So, these books may be snatched up for a satisfying, quick read over the hurried morning coffee or savored, many at a time, feet up in front of the fire with a good single malt.

—Rick Durden
Aviation attorney, CFII, ATP, Douglas DC-3 and Cessna Citation type ratings, author of hundreds of aviation articles and of *The Thinking Pilot* book series

Ely Air Lines

Select Stories from
10 Years of a Weekly Column

Volume 1 of 2

By Mike Ely and Linda Street-Ely

http://paperairplanepublishing.com

 Published 2020 by Paper Airplane Publishing LLC.
http://paperairplanepublishing.com

Cover concept: Miriam Rue, Waterslide Illustrations
Cover art production: Vickie Swisher, Studio 2020
Mini silhouettes by Miriam Rue and Pasindu Lakshan

ISBN: 978-1-947677-02-9

1. Aviation 2. Pilots 3. Flying 4. Airplanes 5. Mike Ely 6. Linda Street-Ely 7. Ely Air Lines

About the Authors

Mike Ely has logged thousands of hours over more than forty years as a professional pilot. He holds an airline transport pilot certificate with multiple type ratings and a flight instructor certificate. Mike has taught people to fly in small single-engine airplanes, gliders, several types of turboprops, and corporate jets. As a freight pilot and an international corporate pilot, he has flown through all kinds of weather to many places, both exotic and boring. His love for writing was instilled by his father at an early age.

Linda Street-Ely is an award-winning multi-genre author. She also holds an airline transport pilot certificate, a commercial seaplane certificate, and a tailwheel endorsement. She has air raced all over the U.S., including four times in the historic all-women's transcontinental Air Race Classic. Besides flying, Linda has a keen appreciation for great storytelling. She loves to travel the world, meet people, and learn about other cultures because she believes great stories are everywhere.

Together, Linda and Mike are Team Ely, five-time National Champions of the Sport Air Racing League in their Grumman Cheetah, named the *Elyminator* and dubbed "The Fastest Cheetah in the Known Universe." They live in Liberty, Texas.

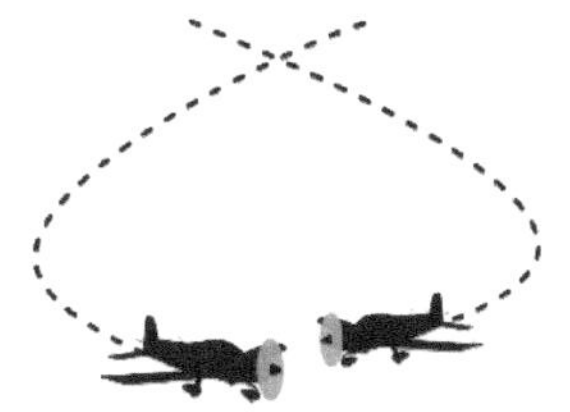

How Flying Stories Happen: A Dedication

We are deeply grateful to Cynthia Smith, owner of the *Liberty Gazette,* for making it possible to share over ten years of aviation stories, as well as informational and educational pieces about airports and their intrinsic and limitless necessity and value. Cynthia has made it easy for a couple of pilots to express their passion for their community and the flying life.

The journey began when the late Kevin Ladd, local historian and author, proposed we write an article about aviation. He pitched the idea to Cynthia, whose father flew B-17s during World War II. We submitted our first piece, and when she accepted, we just couldn't stop.

That first article was written to bring our local airport into the limelight and show our nonflying friends and neighbors the great asset we mustn't take for granted.

We continued each week with informational, uplifting, and motivating stories about airports, pilots, and all of life touched by flying.

These stories are rarely found in general audience publications. We expect to see pieces like these in aviation magazines, but as a newspaper the *Liberty Gazette* stands out as uniquely supporting its entire community and beyond with articles about people, events, and even airports.

Therefore, we dedicate this book to Cynthia Smith, without whom it would not exist; and also to our readers, to those who have graciously shared their stories, and to all the great lovers of flight we've met living this life of aerial adventure.

TABLE OF CONTENTS

Volume 1 of 2

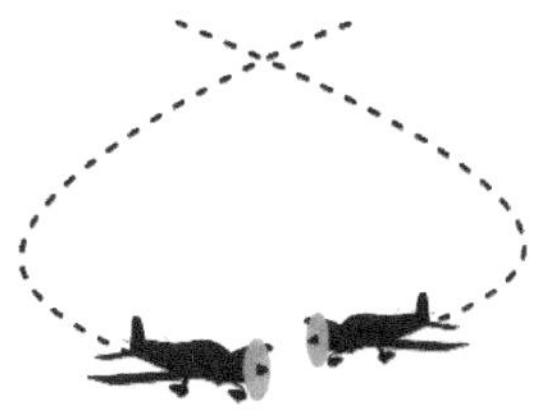

Introduction

Ely Air Lines, a column first titled "The View from Up Here," debuted in the *Liberty Gazette* on June 26, 2007. Prompted to bring attention to our community airport in a positive way, we offered reports and commentary from our corner of the sky over Liberty County, Texas.

We aimed to inform and delight readers by telling stories about interesting people, places, and great adventures and to educate the nonflying public on the importance of having an airport. Liberty, Texas, is one of the fortunate cities, and all the good that comes from having an airport is something we want our neighbors—and the world—to know.

In celebrating the first ten years of Ely Air Lines, we sifted through over five hundred stories and selected one hundred for this book series. These pieces represent a variety of ways in which aviation touches all our lives. They are accounts of some of the most inspiring, yet ordinary people whose stories come from as close as our back door to as far away and diverse as Paris and Congo.

In these pages you will read of young and old, male and female, and people of many nationalities, attesting to the wide reach of aviation. Here are the faces of the beauty of the flying world – the champions who make this a better place. They are the honorable, humble, heroic, and sometimes the humorous.

We also share our flying adventures from excursions and races in our Grumman Cheetah, which we named the *Elyminator*, to soaring in gliders, trips in jets, and flipping fun in aerobatic airplanes.

We hope you enjoy these samplings of the first ten years as much as we enjoyed writing them.

Blue skies,
Mike & Linda
Ely Air Lines

There Will Come a Time

A single lifetime, even though entirely devoted to the sky, would not be enough for the study of so vast a subject. A time will come when our descendants will be amazed that we did not know things that are so plain to them.

—Seneca, *Natural Questions, Book 7,* first century CE

About Flying

Mike: Whether your type is stick-'n-rudder, cyclic and collective, kerosene burner, quiet glider, full of hot air, or a ground-bound lover of aviation, Ely Air Lines has for over a decade been the place for aviation stories from everywhere.

The average age of today's student pilot is thirty-two. The average actively flying private pilot is forty-five, and many over fifty find that it's the right time to fulfill their lifelong ambition to fly.[1]

What draws us to aviation? The view, for one thing. Experiencing the altitude dimension means your world is no longer flat, and we humans are attracted to fullness. Flying gives us an experience of fullness in a whole new way, a perspective on the world denied when gravity isn't defied.

Linda: And how about the satisfaction that comes with challenge and accomplishment—the hunt and the capture? No matter how long ago it may have been, aviators remember their first solo flight, from the moment the instructor stepped out of the airplane and cleared the way for the student to say,

[1] General Aviation Manufacturers Association *2016 General Aviation Statistical Databook and 2017 Industry Outlook*, https://gama.aero/wp-content/uploads/2016-GAMA-Databook_forWeb.pdf

"I made that airplane fly—me, the boss, the pilot-in-command." And yet we knew there was so much more to learn.

Mike: There will always be someone who has flown more hours, larger aircraft, higher, faster, or longer. Yet stories from novice pilots are just as exciting, and that's the fun we have in these air lines—the people, the adventures... Oh, the places we can go!

Linda: And so, aviation nuts, propeller heads, jetti-sons, rotor rats, and glider guys and gals, here's to a future that includes some measure of aerial awesomeness. You can always go out to your local airport and say hello to whoever's around while you watch for airplanes.

Give me a mile of highway and I can travel a mile;
give me a mile of runway and I can go anywhere.

—Author unknown

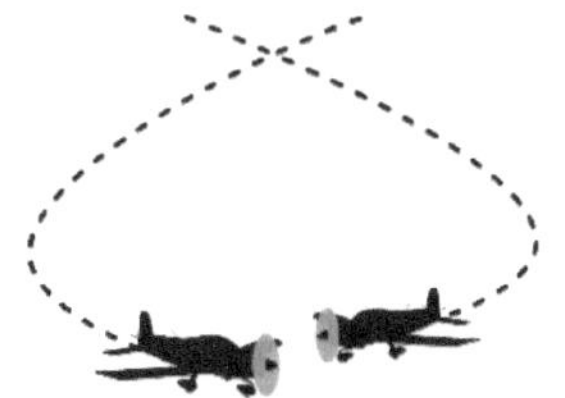

Who We Are, How We Got Here

Linda: I went to an air show at Ellington Field because I wanted something to do, not because I was interested in airplanes. It had been almost two years since I lost my husband and our two youngest children and all we owned in a house fire. I had to force myself to get out of bed each day. This air show would get me outside and if only for a little while, might help distract my grieving mind.

As I watched the aerobatic pilots perform their daring maneuvers, I thought, *I wonder what it would be like to do that.* Later, as I admired the aerial D-Day reenactment honoring our veterans, that thought returned. A little while later, when the USAF Thunderbirds displayed their finesse, I had that same idea again, but this time it was with a conviction to rival the power of an F-16 surprising the crowd with a low approach from behind.

Wow! I wonder what it'd be like to do that!

That was October 16, 2004. Two weeks later, I found myself in the left seat of a Cessna 152. Anthony Schreiber, the eager flight instructor by my side, talked me through the takeoff roll on Ellington Airport's 9,001-foot runway, One Seven Right. I studied and flew every chance I had, and on May 16, 2005, I flew with FAA designated pilot examiner Cliff Hyde, Jr. and earned my private pilot certificate.

What the gift of flying has done for me is immeasurable. It is a gift from God, who knew I needed something new and different—with no painful memories attached—to give me a zest for life. Some people have assumed I get this "closer-to-heaven" feeling when flying, healing my soul. But that's not it.

What flying did first was divert my attention to a new challenge, one that required my full attention. One does not get over the death of a spouse and children. We who have grieved these losses know we must learn how to walk with our wounds. In healthy grieving, we develop this new walk. Over time, flying became the way I have taken many steps.

Nearly two years after I began private pilot flight training, I fell in love with a career pilot. Mike and I married in September 2006. He said goodbye to his international chief pilot job in Florida and came to live with me in Texas.

We thought we'd like to share our stories of the wonderful adventures in aviation. This is what we pilots call hangar flying.

Mike says lots of hangar flying stories start out, "There I was, flat on my back at thirty thousand feet..." That comes from a 1987 book by aviator and humorist Bob Stevens, titled *There I was...flat on my back.* We hope our passion for aviation will be contagious as we encourage you to join us in this flying addiction through stories of adventure off the ground.

Mike: My adventures in the air began when I was fifteen and took my first airplane ride at Chino Airport in California. The ride included aerobatics as part of the package. I was fascinated with flight long before that, when I would watch every airplane that came over our house through my dad's binoculars. I was the proverbial "kid at the airport fence," searching the skies and dreaming of the day that I would be in those cockpits, at those controls. The blame for wear and tear on the binoculars rested on me, making a new pair one of the best birthday presents of my childhood.

I loved airplanes, any airplane. I still do. I guess you could say I was a different kind of bird-watcher as I studied to learn every type of airplane, challenging myself to identify them on sight.

I knew I wanted to fly. Mom, however, had other plans. Hoping to squelch my interest in this "dangerous" activity, she agreed to let me take an airplane ride. Her plan backfired. My brother's friend took me up in an aerobatic trainer. We did loops, rolls, and anything but straight and level—and the kid from the airport fence was hooked.

With four children to raise, my parents could not afford flying lessons, so I worked at various jobs to pay for my training. I earned my private pilot's certificate before I bought my first car. Studying when I couldn't afford to fly, learning from technical books, aviation novels, and hangar flying with other pilots, I became a sponge for anything flying-related.

Although progress seemed slow, every moment spent immersed in aviation has been priceless in my flying career. I love what I do, and this passion for flying has rewarded me greatly with adventures of my childhood dreams.

A pilot's logbook is a storybook of experiences only the grandest of adventure novels could even hope to conjure up. From stories of North Atlantic crossings to flights to South

America to a hop around the patch at Liberty Municipal Airport, every flight emerges as an adventure. A passion for aviation still rises in this globe-spanning corporate pilot, once the kid at the airport fence.

Linda: That passion for aviation has built America's adventure highways, her airport system, which plays a vital role in the health and well-being of every community. In the great state of Texas alone, there are almost four hundred public-use airports, over twenty thousand registered aircraft, and nearly fifty thousand certificated pilots representing over two and a quarter million hours flown each year by general aviation aircraft.[2]

With general and commercial aviation combined, the industry provides about 771,000 jobs in the Lone Star State.[3] Ancillary services also enrich local economies, including aircraft maintenance and avionics shops, aircraft sales, concessions, and many other non-aviation activities. Employment, capital investment, gross sales, and visiting aircraft contribute generously to our economic output.

General aviation pilots and passengers spend money for various goods and services. Besides these measurable benefits, general aviation enhances the quality of life, health, welfare, and safety of citizens by providing the means for transporting goods and engaging in vital services.

If not for America's general aviation airports, neither Mike nor I would have learned to fly, and nor would many airline

---

[2] General Aviation Manufacturers Association, *2016 General Aviation Statistical Databook and 2017 Industry Outlook*, https://gama.aero/wp-content/uploads/2016-GAMA-Databook_forWeb.pdf

[3] http://ftp.dot.state.tx.us/pub/txdot-info/avn/tx_econ_tech.pdf

pilots. Community airports need community support as much as communities need airports. That kid at the airport fence indulging his fantasies with a toy airplane or extending his arms, banked at a thirty-degree angle, running in a figure eight with the roar of a thousand-horsepower engine blowing furiously past his lips, almost convinces even those passing by when he exclaims, "Look at me, Daddy! I'm an airplane!"

Firsts

Mike: The firsts of every pilot's flying history are moments that change us forever. As I took control for the first time of an aircraft leaving the ground, breaking from gravity's grip, achieving that takeoff, my senses were flooded. I had imagined, created, and lived this moment in my dreams. Once a reality, I went through an inner transformation. Upon that first landing, feeling the bump as the wheels connected with the runway, there was no uncertainty in what I wanted to do with my life. When I flew that first solo flight, having graduated from my instructor's constant presence and took dominion over the airborne craft, it made me feel triumphant.

The moment the FAA designated examiner said, "Congratulations, you are now a private pilot," I joined a special group of people who had aspired to the right to make that claim and worked to win it. Finally, in the company of my first passenger, I proved my skill to the world. I was a pilot—it could not be denied—and my heart soared higher than an altimeter ever could.

Like all worthy adventures, these high points were built upon smaller challenges and obstacles that I overcame. Sometimes doubt interrupted. But if learning to fly was easy, what kind of adventure would *that* be?

We cherish our firsts, but with time, details fade from memory. A pilot builds chapters of the story with each logbook entry. I hold dear the treasure trove of chronicles and from it can relive my growth, reminding myself of struggles and rejoice in my conquests.

My instructor, Dennis Reece, and I had been practicing touch-and-go landings when he asked me to make the next one a full stop. As we taxied clear of the runway, we pulled over next to the gas pumps. Dennis slid back the canopy of the four-seat Grumman Traveler and asked me for my student pilot certificate and logbook. After scratching out his signature on both, he climbed out and said, "Three times around the patch, and I'll meet you back at the trailer. Just remember what you've learned, enjoy the moment, and have fun."

I radioed the air traffic control tower to get my taxi clearance. It felt different from all the times I had done it before. I had a sense of both fear and excitement as I rolled toward El Monte Airport's Runway One Niner and prepared for takeoff. My heart was beating fast as I advanced the throttle and accelerated down the runway. The airplane seemed to leap into the air and scream skyward with adrenaline of its own. I noticed how significantly better the little Grumman performed without Dennis's weight, and I climbed to pattern altitude quicker than I expected. I followed all the procedures I was taught, making my way around the airport's rectangular pattern by myself for the first time. *You've got an audience,* I thought.

As the main landing gear squeaked onto the runway pavement, accomplishment and triumph welled up in me and burst forth, making it impossible to wipe the grin from my face.

Back on the ground, I was elated at having achieved this special feat. As I parked the airplane and climbed out, Dennis sauntered up, scissors in hand. In keeping with tradition, he cut the back of my shirt and signed and dated the cut piece.

My solo shirt was polyester. It made me sweat even when I wasn't flying solo. Losing part of it was no disappointment because the hole at my back signified that I was now a real pilot.

That was March 7, 1977; I had a whole twenty-three hours of flight time in my logbook.

Adorning the walls of flight schools across the country is evidence of those who faced the challenge and persevered. Sweaty-backed shirttails hang alongside photographs—some dingy and cracked with age—signed and dated by flight instructors who knew, even if the students did not, that they were ready to make that next big leap.

For years, my solo shirttail hung with others that plastered the walls of the old mobile home that El Monte Skyways used as its office building. All of that has long since disappeared, but the memory of that magic moment remains.

My first passenger was my dad. We lived in the Los Angeles area, and what he loved about flying was the visibility above the smog. We stayed in the local area that day. As is customary, I circled over our house to show him what it looked like from the air. He taught me to take shallow banks with first-time passengers because, he said carefully, they might feel like they will fall out. I heeded his advice, and he returned to fly with me on many quests after that.

Mom first flew with me years later, long after I had earned my commercial pilot certificate. She had always been afraid of flying and had not yet flown in a small airplane. That first time, she brought along a family friend whose father was a pilot. After that, Mom flew with me on a couple of grand voyages and she accepted my chosen career.

Family and friends supported me not only in words but in a willingness to take off with me on those early escapades. Introducing the world of flight and sharing our passion brings great joy to a pilot. Our skills are acknowledged. The time and effort we put into learning feels validated and increases the value of having learned to fly with moments that change us forever.

Linda: I am honored to say my first passenger was the late Dr. Jimmie L. Clemmons, or, as he preferred, Brother Jim, pastor of North Main Baptist Church in Liberty. Learning to fly when my life had been turned upside down by severe tragedy gave me something to focus on, something new to help my mind work again.

Family and friends were instrumental in that journey. Many came to celebrate my newly granted certificate at my "pilot party." Shortly after, Brother Jim said he would love to take a ride with me some time. He'd ask, "When're we going up?" And he hinted several times, "I love to fly."

Brother Jim was well-known in our community for his genuine love and concern for others. He was one of my strongest encouragers during that difficult time following the fatal house fire. It seemed fitting he would be the first person to ride with me when I became a certificated pilot and the doors opened for a new life.

I was eager to fly with my first passenger, so we set a date to meet at Ellington Field where I would rent a Cessna 172 and take him on a scenic flight around the area. I remembered my instructor, Anthony, saying my best flight would be when I take my first passenger. How I hoped he would be right.

After completing the preflight inspection, buckling in my passenger, and handing him a headset, I continued down the checklist. We use checklists because every detail is too important to miss.

With my feet on the brakes, I flipped the master switch on and shouted out the open window, "Clear prop!"

Turn the key, push the mixture in, and listen for the engine to catch. It started right up. I adjusted the RPMs, then turned on the navigation equipment and set the radios to Ellington's ground control and tower frequencies. I listened to the recorded weather briefing before requesting permission to taxi.

The ground controller sent us to One Seven Right at intersection Bravo. There I stopped to perform various tests of the airplane, a procedure called the runup. I checked my flight instruments, valves, and selectors. "Fuel selector on 'both,' mixture rich..." Checking the yoke, ailerons, and rudders, I confirmed, "Flight controls free and clear."

Running the RPMs up to 1800, I checked both right and left magnetos, and then double-checked our seatbelts, shoulder harnesses, and door latches. Everything looked good, so I called the tower. "Ellington Tower, Cessna 72566 on Bravo holding short of One Seven Right, ready for departure."

Brother Jim was as excited and encouraging as my dad would have been if he were still with us. He smiled and gave me the thumbs-up when we heard, "Cessna 72566, wind calm, Runway One Seven Right, cleared for takeoff."

My feet danced lightly on the rudder pedals as I guided the plane down the runway centerline. We lifted into the sky. It was a beautiful day.

Since Ellington is so close to the airspace belonging to Houston's Hobby Airport to the north, we flew south for a bird's-eye view of the Gulf of Mexico. Above the shops, the amusement park, and the boats docked at Kemah, I was pleased to see Brother Jim truly enjoying the flight.

Over the beaches of Galveston, then on toward Smith Point, we both pointed out familiar sights and talked about how different things look from the air. Time passed too quickly, and soon we had to return to the airport.

Inbound over La Porte, I radioed Ellington Tower. The controller gave me a squawk code in reply, which I entered into the transponder so our plane would show up on the tower's radar. He instructed me to enter left base for One Seven Right and report two miles. It didn't take long to get there. Winds were light and variable, and the pattern wasn't busy so he cleared me to land right away. Easy. No crabbing or crosswind corrections to show off for my first passenger. *It should be a smooth landing.*

Anthony was right. It was the smoothest landing I'd ever made. Brother Jim told everyone he couldn't even tell that we had touched the ground, which was probably an exaggeration, but one appreciated by a new pilot.

Given our history, it was especially meaningful that Brother Jim was my first passenger—the man God sent to minister to me a few years earlier.

A year later, family and close friends converged on North Main Baptist Church where Mike and I married, and Brother

Jim officiated. Someone decorated the church with radio-controlled airplanes, and our sweet friend LaDell made a runway cake for our reception. Addressing our guests, Brother Jim mentioned the plane ride and talked about new life and purpose:

> *Not long ago, Linda had gotten her private pilot license and she had invited me to ride with her for the first time. And we left that airport and we were flying across Galveston. And I saw her so meticulously flying, but I also saw an escape. I saw a woman that had found something that had taken her mind; the heavens, the clouds, the area itself seemed to have dissipated the thoughts that would control her mind at that time.*
>
> *And I was so grateful that she had found that: an escape, a reason, something to look forward to. Little would I know that in that escape, she would find Mike. So, all of this has meaning, all of this has purpose. As difficult as the last four years has been for many here, and will always be, today is a new beginning. Today, new life; new hope – especially for you, Linda, new Life.*

Brother Jim is gone now, but his friendship is a gift that will remain with me for eternity. Indeed, there are moments that change a pilot forever. While flying my first passenger let me prove my skill to the world, that flight is tightly clenched in my heart.

Givin' 'Em the Business

Nowadays a businessman can go from his office straight to the airport, get into his airplane and fly six hundred or seven hundred miles without taking off his hat. He probably will not even mention this flight, which a bare twenty-five years ago would have meant wearing leather jacket and helmet and goggles and risking his neck every minute of the way.

No, he probably wouldn't mention it – except to another flier. Then they will talk for hours. They will re-create all the things seen and felt in that wonderful world of air: the sense of remoteness from the busy world below, the feeling of intense brotherhood formed with those who man the radio ranges and control towers and weather stations that bring the pilot home, the clouds and the colors, the surge of the wind on their wings.

They will speak of things that are spiritual and beautiful and of things that are practical and utilitarian; they will mix up angels and engines, sunsets and spark plugs, fraternity and frequencies in one all-encompassing comradeship of interests that makes for the best and most lasting kind of friendship any man can have.

– Percy Knauth, *Wind on My Wings*, 1960

Liberty Airport's Humble Beginnings

We wanted to tell the story of the beginnings of the Liberty Municipal Airport. That is, not a story only about an airport, but about a community made up of pilots who flew out of this airport in its formative days. While doing so, it was most important to hold true to the passion and ideals that were instrumental in building that airport community.

One might wonder if writer Percy Knauth had ever been to Liberty, Texas, and knew some of the characters here—Benny, Earl, Patti, Charles. He seems to have described them in his book *Wind on My Wings*. We'll give them a proper introduction.

Benny Rusk

Most of the land where the airport is today was once the property of Benny Rusk. But he didn't have an easy start.

His father had worked for Humble Oil Company in nearby Baytown. Missing his home in Nacogdoches and longing for the farming life again, when the price of cotton climbed to thirty cents, Benny's dad left Humble Oil to farm cotton. The next year, the price of cotton plunged to five cents. Those were the tough times. They never went hungry, but they ate a lot of cornbread.

One of six children, Benny began milking cows at age five and farmed until he was eighteen. The two years he worked at a shipyard before being drafted probably caused his hearing loss that disqualified him from flying for the Navy, his first choice.

From the Army's Camp Wolters, he was shipped off to Europe during World War II. He was boots on the ground in four major battles, including the Battle of the Bulge, and finished his time in Berlin with the 82nd Airborne. After one year, eleven months, and twenty-three days, Benny collected only three paychecks. He dismissed the lack of pay with, "They moved me so much, I guess they couldn't find me."

But the cashier job at the First State Bank in Liberty was a good move, as he would later work his way up to bank president.

Farmer, war veteran, banker, and soon-to-be pilot, Benny arrived in Liberty at a pivotal time for aviation. It was 1953. Rice farming ruled in Liberty County, and Benny learned quickly that you have to be careful what you say because everyone here is related.

Earl Atkins

During the heyday of rice production in Southeast Texas, a former World War II instructor pilot named Earl Atkins was flying for M&M Air Service, seeding and crop dusting from 175 small grass and dirt airstrips in the area. One of these was Roy House's airfield, across the Trinity River on the west side of Liberty, north of Highway 90.

Earl wanted more space than he had at Roy's airfield, so he formed Atkins Flying Service and went looking for a place big enough to grow his business. That's when he met banker Benny Rusk.

Benny had forty-two acres in nearby Ames, but if he could acquire more, Earl would move his spray operation there. He would offer flight training, crop dusting, aircraft sales, and charter service.

Benny knew aviation was vital to a community's health, and the area needed an airport. With skillful negotiation and planning and a great passion for aviation, he acquired twelve more acres from a neighbor. Then he bought five hundred feet of frontage road from another neighbor. This was enough for a landing strip. Benny and Earl built hangars, and Atkins Flying Service moved in.

Benny leased the fifty-eight acres to Earl, and Earl taught Benny to fly. A lifelong friendship formed between them. By 1958, Earl bought the property from Benny, intending to build it up into a full-fledged airport.

The Instructor

Earl was a top-notch pilot, and Benny had stories to prove it, such as the way he handled an airplane while crop dusting. Rather than make sweeping turns at the end of each row, Earl would pull the nose up almost vertical, kick the rudder, and the resulting hammerhead—an aerobatic maneuver—would pivot the plane nose-down, picking up speed. He'd ease it back to level, in line with the next row. "He cut those turn times in half," which still made Benny laugh sixty years later.

But one time the control stick detached, coming out in Earl's hand right after takeoff. He dumped his eighteen-hundred-pound load, used the trim tab for pitch control, and made power adjustments to get the airplane down safely.

The Student

If he was going to learn to fly, Benny would need an airplane. Houston television personality Ben Erskine agreed to rent his Luscombe to Benny for $3.50 an hour. After four hours of lessons, Benny bought a 1949 Cessna 170 from the military aero club at Ellington Air Force Base in Houston. He paid $2,900 and sold it a year later for the same price. The only money he spent on it was for a new tire.

He claimed his only mishap came after he had many hours logged in multiple airplanes. It was a belly landing in a retractable gear aircraft that occurred when a passenger was playing with the controls. Benny didn't realize the passenger had retracted the landing gear.

There was that time, though, as his wife, Linda, reminded him that they were returning from a trip to her parents' home when ice built up on their Cessna 310. This made the airplane heavy and altered the aerodynamics. Fortunately, they were over Eagle Lake Airport. But Linda recalled, "He had to land the airplane by looking at what little bit he could see out the side window because ice covered the front."

Earl had taught Benny to assess any situation he encountered and look for solutions that may not be obvious. But most important, to fly the plane. Benny credited Earl's teaching as the reason he landed safely that day, able to fly again. "Every moment has been worth it. We take risks every day, but you can see things from up there you never dreamed were there."

Business Aviation

Benny also appreciated Earl's business savvy. "Art Barkis's dad," he explained, "held the patent on some oilfield machinery. When Art came for flying lessons, Earl explained to his dad how airplanes could increase business by cutting down the sales staff's travel time."

The men struck a deal whereby Earl would purchase a Twin Beech and provide charter service to the elder Mr. Barkis. His sales staff covered more ground in less time, and he credited Earl for tripling his business.

That's the thing about business aviation. It pays for itself many times over. Benny saw this when he took bank clients to his ranch in West Texas.

"It'd take twelve to thirteen hours to drive the five hundred ninety-five miles from Liberty to the ranch. But we had a Comanche 400 that could make the trip out there in two hours and forty minutes. With the wind at our back, we could do it in two hours and fifteen minutes. An airplane puts one more day on the week."

He chuckled and pointed out the window toward the airstrip behind his house. "We'd leave late on a Friday from that strip and be back on Monday morning before anyone knew we were gone."

Charles Wiggins and How to Advertise Your Grocery Store

Charles Wiggins was another businessman who frequented the airport. His earliest memory of the notion of flight was seeing a biplane fly low over his family's house. He was just a little tyke, didn't even know anything about airplanes, but he said he'd like to fly that. From time to time he would think of that biplane, and when he reached his teen years, he scraped together what he could to get flying lessons.

He soloed in a J-3 Cub, but he couldn't afford to finish training before starting college at Sam Houston State University. Then he was drafted into the Army.

After he was discharged in the mid-1960s, he and his brother acquired Wiggins Grocery, which their parents had built in 1947. The business was doing well thanks in large part to Wiley Smith, who started what is now the *Liberty Gazette* newspaper.

In the *Gazette,* Wiggins Grocery could get printed coupons in the hands of residents and spread the word about their business. "Wiley gave us the first couple of full-page ads and, once we advertised, our little neighborhood store grew and grew."

The increased business that advertising brought enabled Charles to restart flight training. Mr. Frazier, who crop dusted for Earl, took Charles on as a student in a Cessna 150. After earning his private pilot certificate, he bought his first two airplanes, an Aeronca Chief and then a Citabria.

The more time he logged, the more he wanted to share his love of flight. If only he could show more people how flying makes you feel.

The idea came quickly. In their grocery store advertising, the Wiggins brothers added an invitation to fly. "I loved sharing the adventure and wonder of flight, so we'd put in our ads: 'Come fly with us!' People loved it! They shopped with us and then flew with us. It made such a difference in our business that soon we were knocking out walls and enlarging."

The Liberty Airport Becomes Municipal

Earl had done what he set out to do. He built an airport that was serving the community by offering agricultural services to Liberty County farmers. The airport gave business leaders—like Art Barkis in the oilfield and Charles Wiggins in the grocery business—an edge over their competitors.

It also gave Liberty an advantage over neighboring towns. Emergency services could easily access the city by air. It was time to draw in the nonflying neighbors, to let them know about the airport's important contributions. Earl would introduce them to the fun side of aviation.

The Civil Air Patrol sponsored the first air show in Liberty in 1969. Benny said five thousand people attended. "Near the end, a man and woman asked Earl to take them up, one on each wing, so they could parachute down. I wasn't sure how they would jump off the wing. But right in front of the crowd at eight hundred fifty feet, the minimum altitude they needed for the chutes to open, Earl suddenly cut back the throttle, almost like stopping the plane in midair. The two went sailing forward and opened their chutes. The crowd loved it."

Earl had enjoyed a successful aviation business on his private strip, but he could envision the greater benefit for all. He had not only built an airport, but cultivated local support, too. Residents and politicians seemed to understand the great value. The following year, Earl gave the airport to the City of Liberty. An official dedication ceremony brought another air show. The city provided barbecue. People brought lawn chairs and delighted in performances by aerobatic pilots, parachute jumpers, and sailplanes.

Earl would continue to manage the airport and run his business until he moved to McAllen in the Rio Grande Valley. Huey Crouch took over as airport manager. The airport was now a public asset but unfortunately, after a few years, it took a back seat to other city functions.

When support dwindled, the Liberty Civil Air Patrol disbanded and the squadron moved thirty miles south to Baytown. The airport had entered a downswing, but it would bounce back. Meanwhile, there was a surprise in store for Earl.

Patti Is the Girl for Earl

One day, Benny asked his friend Patti Shannon if she would join him on a double date that evening. He wanted her to meet Earl Atkins. That dinner date was the beginning of a new life for Patti.

As she accompanied Earl on his aerial jaunts, he insisted she learn to fly. But Patti only wanted to learn how to land—"you know, in case of an emergency." That made little sense to Earl. Patti would learn to fly. She started out in Charles Wiggins's Citabria, but life brought many interruptions.

Earl and Patti married in 1986 and following their island-hopping honeymoon in the Bahamas, she joined him in McAllen. However, Earl wouldn't agree to her flying anything other than a Citabria until she finished her private pilot training. He wanted her to master the airplane, including stalls, spins, and inverted flight. He believed in her and would be a staunch supporter.

Back in Liberty County, while visiting her folks in Hull, Patti called on Charles and explained her plight. She needed to borrow his Citabria again to finish her private certificate requirements so she could fly other airplanes. Charles agreed and Patti flew the plane down to their home in the valley.

She mastered the Citabria and Earl happily gave her access to more airplanes while she took the next step: instrument training. This teaches pilots how to fly when there is little or no reference to the horizon due to clouds, mist, fog, smoke, darkness, or other conditions. Instrument students learn how to use the airplane's gauges to fly safely even in low visibility.

This requires intense focus, so it's impressive that Patti took her instrument, commercial, and multi-engine checkrides all in one. That's normally three different checkrides. But by then, she had been flying complex aircraft: DC-3s, Navajos, a Cessna 411, and more under Earl's tutelage.

Charles was impressed. "They asked if she could use my Citabria to learn in. The next thing I knew, I hear Patti's flying a Lockheed Constellation across the country!"

Someone with Patti's experience could be full of ego, but she's not. She graciously redirects the attention. "I flew with such great guys that anyone could fly those airplanes. You couldn't mess up, and they really wanted me to do it."

Her personality likely made them eager to teach her how to fly all those airplanes, but she simply responds, "You know it's the really good pilots who want you to love flying as much as they do—they want to share what they love."

With "only a few thousand hours," Patti has dropped jumpers, flown freight, and handled the stress of performing in numerous *Tora! Tora! Tora!* air show reenactments, flying a Super DC-3, which was a wedding present.

"After we married, Earl said, 'Come with me to Beaumont; I have a wedding present for you.'" She laughed while explaining it. "That thing was a mess! It had been in a storm, and the instruments were hanging out. There were holes in it, and one engine was off."

Most chicks would not be diggin' this kind of wedding present. But Patti graciously looked forward to the adventure.

Earl insisted she fly her Cessna 172 back to the valley, and he would fix up the DC-3 enough to get it back home.

Patti would want it repainted, too. "It had the name *Doris* painted on it. That's a big deal to have an airplane named after you."

Earl landed the wedding present with only one engine running. Patti met him on the ramp with a bottle of champagne, and they christened the battered flying machine *Patti*. After the repairs were made, *Patti* was painted on, replacing *Doris*.

The memories brought out a grin when she said, "There isn't much room at the Liberty Airport to take off in a Super DC-3. I had to get all the way back and start my takeoff roll in the grass."

Besides the Citabria, the C-172, the DC-3, Navajo, Cessna 411, and the Super Constellation, Patti has logged time in many vintage aircraft: the Twin Beech, Martin B-26 Marauder, Boeing B-17 Flying Fortress, North American B-25 Mitchell, Boeing Stearman, and a World War I airplane called a Moth Minor. If you go to an air show, you may see some of these airplanes on display in all their glory, including the *Tora! Tora! Tora!* aircraft performing their demonstration of World War II airpower.

Earl and Patti came back to Liberty often, encouraging investment in the airport. In 1991, they organized another air show to celebrate the airport's renovation, which fit nicely with Earl's surprise seventieth birthday party. They brought in vintage aircraft, parachute jumpers, and hosted tours of the airport with its new hangars and extended 3,800-foot runway. The good times were back, but the city's interest would wane and grow like labor pains for many years.

After Earl passed away, Patti eventually sold the aviation business in McAllen and returned to Liberty County. And while she says she doesn't necessarily miss performing at air shows or flying cargo into Mexico, she stays in touch with her aviation buddies.

Charles Inverted

That Citabria Charles loaned to Patti had a 150-horsepower engine, an inverted fuel system, and a smoke system. It was great for aerobatic maneuvers (and it's Airbatic spelled backward) because with smoke on, you could fly a maneuver and take a look at how you did by checking the trail.

On the seventy-fifth anniversary of the Wright Brothers' first flight, Charles wanted to do something to celebrate. He and a friend decided they would fly inverted as long as they could. The Citabria's inverted tank only holds about a gallon of fuel, but their safety belts pulled hard against their collarbones and across their hips, and blood rushed to their heads. Before they could burn through that small amount of fuel, they realized it lasted longer than they cared to stay inverted.

After many hours of fun in the Citabria, it was time to graduate to something bigger.

Charles discovered a disassembled Ryan PT-22 in a widow's garage in Vidor, Texas. The lady wanted $500 for anything aviation-related in the garage, so Charles grabbed a friend to help gather it all up.

"We pulled the car around to this old shed, and we had to kick the trash out of the way to get to it. We get inside, and there are airplane parts everywhere, and a Ranger engine suspended from a hoist. Half the crate was sitting below the engine, and the other half we'd already kicked aside! There were almost enough parts for two airplanes, but there was only one engine and it was hanging in the air."

Three trips with a huge trailer emptied the lady's garage. He thought he'd part out the plane, but his plans changed the next month when he saw an aviation magazine article about John Gotchoff, who specialized in rebuilding PT-22s. Charles called and explained his acquisition and John replied, "Just so happens I'm delivering a PT-22 to Galveston. I'll stop and take a look."

John made his airplane delivery, got a truck, and drove ninety miles north to Liberty. Upon careful inspection, he offered to build Charles a PT-22 from all the parts, in exchange for the Ranger engine and $5,000. They agreed on the deal and spent the next day cramming parts into every little space of that truck. It took about a year to rebuild the airplane.

The PT-22 was the model that held the speed record for snap rolls until the modern jet fighter era, when the wings were engineered to increase the roll rate. Charles called it a neck-snapping experience. "The wings were built like a bridge—solid. Some of the people who had worked on Charles Lindbergh's *Spirit of St. Louis* were still working for

Ryan Aeronautical Company when they started the PT-22 project."

This model, which reminded him of a warthog (the animal, not the airplane), had a sad history. Several had been delivered to the U.S. Army Air Corps on December 1, 1941, for a summer flight training program. Once the U.S. went to war, the PT-22 was found to be unsuitable for primary training, so the Army used the PT-19 and Stearman, and the PT-22s became surplus.

One concern was that the cylinder arrangement caused an irregular beat. Friends listening from the ground and passengers were often alarmed because it sounded like engine trouble. Charles soon learned that if he was practicing stalls, it could look like engine trouble, too.

"Compared to the Citabria, the PT-22 flew like a brick. You couldn't stall it and expect to recover in less than fifteen hundred feet."

Then he laughed, thinking of the first time he rolled the PT-22. "I had stuff in my shirt pockets I forgot to take out. The PT-22 is an open-cockpit airplane, and suddenly I see stuff just falling out everywhere as I go into the roll." He said if you tried calling him back then and he didn't return your call, it was probably because the number was on one of those pieces of paper.

Benny's Gallery

Down the hallway of Benny's modest farm home were many framed photos hanging on the walls. Some were from his boxing days as a heavyweight contender from 1946 to 1948. One was a picture of the time he fought the heavyweight champion contender, Roy Harris, of Cut-N-Shoot, at the 1958 Trinity Valley Exposition. That fight was a big deal in Liberty. The match ended in a draw.

Others were shots of him with airplanes; many from trips he took with his family. There were a few photos of a Curtiss C-46 Commando, once used by the Army Air Corps in World War II to fly the "Hump" from India to China. The picture was taken when he and Earl Atkins picked up the airplane in Alaska and flew it back to McAllen.

But Benny especially liked the picture of a Northrop T-38 Talon, a supersonic trainer jet used by the U.S. Air Force. He flew it for an hour, taking turns with his friends Charles Wiggins and folk singer Gordon Lightfoot. That hour was a thrill ride, he said. "The power provided by the jet's afterburners shot us straight up to fourteen thousand feet. It flies even better upside down!"

Afterward, when someone asked him what he thought of the T-38, Benny couldn't hide his enthusiasm. "I think every family should have one!"

Reflection

The first time we visited the Liberty Municipal Airport, there were no fences. It felt as though we had driven onto a vacant lot east of town. There were a few airplanes tied down near the two old, rusty-looking orange hangars and the old, but still-in-use, fuel tank. Anyone and everyone had access to this public asset.

A week later, we discovered that the TSA had made their presence known. A new perimeter fence blocked off most of the runway, taxiway, and hangars from all but a privileged few who received a code from the city. It seemed this airport's golden days were lost, when anyone could walk up and look at real airplanes.

The best way to bring people into the aviation community is to make them feel welcome. That fence said just the opposite. Its very presence threatened the fifty-eight-acre airport that had held sentinel here since 1956. The message it shouted was the opposite of the image Earl and Patti Atkins, Benny Rusk, Charles Wiggins, and many others invested so much in creating.

After the fence encircled the property, the airport languished for a time. As we wrote about it week after week in the *Gazette*, interest regenerated. People would approach us and say, "You're the airport people, right? You know, I didn't even know we had an airport until I read about it in the newspaper." The public's renewed knowledge and acceptance—even embrace—of the airport, caused some city officials to have a change of mind.

Hurricane Ike brought disaster in 2008, tearing up the old T-hangars and a few derelict aircraft stored inside them. Some good airplanes were destroyed as well. Since the cleanup, the airport has received a slow progression of improvements.

With matching state funding, the ramp area on the east side was enlarged. The airport received a new fuel farm with the addition of jet fuel, new T-hangars built to much stronger standards, improvements to drainage, and a small pilot lounge.

Thanks to the development and amenities such as jet fuel, during Hurricane Harvey in 2017, the Liberty Municipal Airport hosted the most relief operations on the east side of Houston, with C-130s and other military support aircraft using the airport to its fullest potential, for its highest purpose.

Thank You, Benny and Earl

Earl Atkins is properly credited as the founder of the Liberty Municipal Airport, but it didn't happen without Benny Rusk, a hard-working, humble man who spoke generously of the good in others.

He may not have realized how important his little grass strip would become. When Liberty faces a crisis and roads are jammed or closed, help can come by air. When business people need to fly into Liberty, they have a place to land and contribute to the local economy.

Benny and Earl's passion and enthusiasm not only sparked many friends and family members to learn to fly, but also laid the groundwork for Liberty to become an integral part of the national transportation system, an asset to the community that benefits us in immeasurable ways and will outlast us all.

Airplanes, Adventure, and All That Grabein Jazz

Linda: Swinging to the tunes of the Charlie Gray Band made my heart smile thinking of my dad, who grew up during the Big Band era. "Charlie Gray" was Charles Grabein. He lived a life of service to others with a tremendous sense of adventure. He was a naval photographer, a civilian pilot, a high school music teacher, and a gifted storyteller who regaled us with many tales, a few of which we picked to share.

Mike: Real estate development northwest of downtown Houston hides any trace of the small airfield that once graced the open countryside beyond the city limits. An airplane for sale there beckoned to young Charles and his cousin. The motor ran and the prop turned, but otherwise the little thing was rather ragged. The two student pilots thought it was worth every penny of the $150 they paid to take it home to Conroe, where they would breathe new life into it.

"Fabric was tearing off the wings as I flew it back." Charles chuckled, recalling his introduction to how he learned what's required to keep an airplane in the air. "The wind was blowing, and the rain was coming down so hard that once I landed and came to a full stop, I had to keep the motor running wide open just to stay on the ground."

When the wind stopped, the plane lunged forward. Charles pulled back on the throttle. The engine quit and they couldn't get it to restart, so they towed it to a parking spot on the airport and worked on it.

The high school–aged boys patched their new airplane, flew it some, and sold it when they graduated in 1948.

Linda: Charles went to college, married, and joined the Navy, where he trained as an aerial photographer. He still had only a student pilot certificate and being around airplanes increased his desire to fly. This work gave him incentive when the Navy pilots showed him how to fly their planes once his photo assignments were completed. Eventually, he would have more opportunities, but until then, the Navy had a job for him to do.

In 1952, he was deployed on an aircraft carrier maneuvering in the Pacific near Korea. He was filming incoming aircraft from an upper deck overlooking the flight deck when, in an instant, one came straight at him. Focusing his movie camera, he stepped back instinctively but continued to record the Corsair's landing, which broke off its arresting hook. The out-of-control aircraft careened into a wall, slid along it, and smashed into another wall below him. The crew rushed to the damaged aircraft and pulled the pilot out to safety. Charles had captured the entire harrowing sequence on film.

Another time while stationed in Dallas, Charles was sent on a photo mission over Oklahoma, assigned to take pictures of six Navy jets that were damaged when they flew into a thunderstorm. He accompanied a Navy lieutenant in a Beech 18 to the locations where the jets had landed. Charles took so many photos he used up all the rolls he brought, so they planned to pick up more at an Air Force base on the way back.

When they landed at their interim stop, Charles climbed out to get his supplies, noticing that the pilot headed to the operations building. He assumed the lieutenant had duties to attend to, perhaps filing the next flight plan, ordering fuel, checking weather, or the all-important biological pit stop.

It took a while for supply personnel to fill his order, but finally Charles piled the seven-seat plane up with photo paper, chemicals, and film, filling even the aisle.

Happy with his stash, he awaited the pilot's return. He looked up to see the lieutenant stagger toward the plane, not looking too well. The pilot stumbled into the right seat. Charles, thinking the lieutenant's condition was from drinking—and maybe he would let him fly once they were airborne—climbed into the left seat, ready to go. As they began the takeoff roll, the pilot sputtered, "You have control," and passed out cold.

Still believing the pilot was inebriated, Charles thought, "Okay, I can do this," and continued the takeoff. "I didn't realize we were overweight and out of balance with all that stuff in the back. I managed to get the gear up and since the main wheels move forward when they retract, it helped a little to redistribute that weight. I still had to push almost all the way forward on the control wheel. It felt like the tail was going to fall out from under me, it was so aft-heavy."

When he radioed the base in Dallas, the executive officer ordered him to make a straight-in landing but to keep the gear up and land in the grass. Something inside Charles said *no*. At fifty feet above the ground, he lowered the gear and set the plane down perfectly on the runway. An ambulance arrived for the unconscious pilot.

The next morning, Charles received orders to see the captain. "He read from an official piece of paper, saying I had disobeyed a direct order to land wheels up, but a couple of people wanted to speak before he made his recommendation."

Charles thought he'd be under the brig rather than in it. His chief stood beside him. Then the now-conscious pilot entered the room, followed by the maintenance officer, photographer officer, and the photo lab guys, all of whom came in support of Charles's actions.

The captain stood and read his verdict: "Seaman Charles Grabein, I hereby award you this Letter of Commendation for saving the airplane and this pilot's life."

Hypoglycemia had never been detected in the pilot, so no one knew what was wrong with him when he passed out. The medical condition ended his flying career, but Charles's quick decisions may have saved his life. Charles understood later that the best decision would have been to not take off. Both he and the pilot were fortunate he was able to handle the situation with no experience in that airplane.

Understandably, the controller acted as he did to minimize the danger. He was talking to a guy who was not a fully trained pilot, and this was an emergency situation. The controller would have known that extending the gear in the final seconds before landing could add considerably more stress. Time and focus would have been taken away from making a safe landing. But Charles felt comfortable with the extra workload and made his own decision. By not doing a belly landing, he saved the airplane from damage to the propellers and engines. This allowed the medics reach the sick pilot quicker.

After being honorably discharged following fourteen years of service, Charles went back to school and earned a music degree. He also continued to fly, earning his civilian private pilot certificate. As a high school band director in the 1970s, Charles had summers off and frequently flew from the Liberty airport.

When he turned seventy, he hopped into a K-35 Beechcraft Bonanza, a V-tail. He grinned sheepishly as he described his favorite thing about it. "It's not aerobatic, but you can do it."

He thought he had the mettle of his youth and tried an aerobatic maneuver. "My body came out fine, but my mind didn't." The plane's power was too much, and Charles no longer trusted himself in a high-performance aircraft. He grounded himself from the Bonanza, continuing a few more years in a Citabria until it was time to hang up his wings.

Mike: A good storyteller relives the story. A great one lets his audience live it too. Charles was a breath of fresh air and a joy to listen to, on clarinet and saxophone—and in his storytelling. I treasure our hangar-flying sessions, each one a thrill with wonderful tales of his lifelong love affair with flight. He even swooped his arms, airplane-style, just like I do, when talking about aerial adventures. He was like a self-exciting magneto on a piston-engine airplane.

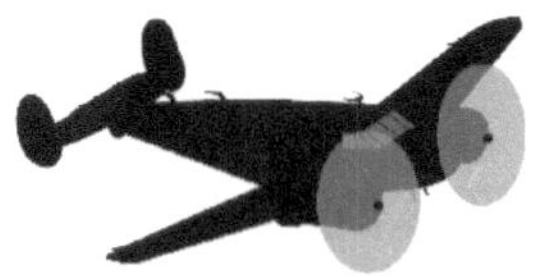

David Rogers – Never Mind the Photos, I've Gone Flying

Mike: On our journeys between Houston's Ellington Field and parts northeast, we regularly crossed over the airstrip labeled *Rogers* on the Houston aeronautical sectional chart. Down among the trees, the east-west-oriented grass strip looked inviting. I spotted three Beech 18 carcasses there. Each time I was over the strip, they reminded me that I needed to learn the story behind those seemingly abandoned ghosts. Besides, I thought it might fit into a novel I was writing.

To land on someone's private airstrip without their permission is not good etiquette. I had to find the owner from the ground. Tracing roads from the air and cross-referencing with a navigation chart, I finally found the property. The gates were locked, so I left a note.

A few days later, David Rogers called. T9A3 was the FAA's official designation for his three-thousand-foot airstrip that ended at Cedar Bayou. Before we took off to land on his strip for the first time, David briefed me about the particulars of his place. The turf was soft along the edges, but the middle was solid ground topped with leftover crushed concrete, making it in good condition for us to touch down. Stay in the middle.

At his invitation, we swooped down in our Cheetah one Sunday afternoon. At the runway's east end was one of the skeletal Beech 18s I'd studied from the sky. We later learned that David bought all three as leftovers, to supply parts for a fourth Beech 18 he bought in 1965. We knew that one of these once belonged to Earl Atkins, and we were eager to find out which one.

We taxied past a swimming pool, a long and substantial building, a large hangar, and a tractor and mower then spun our Cheetah around and shut down. As we hopped down from the wings, David greeted us warmly and led us into the hangar to see his Beech D18S, *sans* engines. The newly rebuilt Pratt & Whitney R-985 engines, 450-horsepower radials, rested on pallets next to the Beech.

Over the next several years, we had the pleasure of getting to know more about him as he filled us in on how he happened to end up in this place, with these airplanes, which wasn't at all what he had planned.

Linda: David studied agricultural education at Sam Houston State University in Huntsville. While bopping around town, he and a buddy discovered a one-pump Humble Oil gas station for sale not far from their dorm. Both boys had worked at gas stations during high school. With $1,200 borrowed from their parents, they bought the station and worked it together. This was the start of the entrepreneurial life of David Rogers.

One day while leafing through his ag studies, he reflected on a scouting trip he'd made a few years earlier in 1950, when he was fourteen. He thought, *What a pivotal time in a boy's life that seems to be.* David thought fondly of his scoutmaster, Bill Kubik, a former paratrooper.

Mr. Kubik had been such a great influence. He had taken the troop to the Philmont Scout Ranch for their hiking merit badge, an experience David felt helped mold him into a better person. As his mind wandered back to that time, he recalled that Mr. Kubik had taken pictures. He wondered if his old scoutmaster might still have those pictures. He'd love to see if he could get copies of them.

Bill Kubik wasn't home when David called, but his wife answered and suggested that David go to the Baytown Airport, where her husband worked as an airplane mechanic.

With the Philmont hiking photos foremost on his mind, David went to the airport in search of Mr. Kubik. The first person he came upon explained that Bill was out flying, but he could make himself at home while waiting for him to return.

There was plenty of activity at the Baytown airport. Airplanes took off and landed. Students took lessons and people flew just for the fun of it. David hadn't seen anything like this before, and all the action made the wait seem inconsequential. He struck up a conversation with pilot John Early, who was fueling his Luscombe. When Mr. Early offered to take David for a ride, the photos were quickly forgotten.

Mike: David was enthralled and began flight training right away. He made his first solo flight in a Piper J-3 Cub. Meanwhile, he acquired another gas station and his entrepreneurial experience grew. The profitable Phillips station he bought in

Huntsville[4] helped keep him in the air. It also afforded him a Cessna 140. By January of 1958, David had earned a private pilot certificate. Soon it was time to move up to a Cessna 170 and get an instrument rating.

When he graduated from college, David sold his gas stations, returning to Baytown to teach fourth grade. But the entrepreneurial spirit cannot be stilled. He bought a Tastee-Freez franchise, which worked out so well that he bought another. This led to real estate development, which led to a variety of endeavors.

Success always came when he found a need and filled it. For example, when he needed concrete for a project, he found it cheaper to buy from the producer and have the raw materials sent to Baytown on a barge up the intercoastal waterway than to have it transported by truck. This saved him a lot of money. When others approached him with similar needs, he included their "orders" along with his next barge load. He bought more concrete and sold it at a much lower price than the competition, still making a handsome profit. And like many efficient business owners, he got around using his airplanes.

By 1965, David was airplane shopping again, this time for a Beechcraft. After briefly considering a Beech Baron, a light twin-engine airplane, the Beech 18 won him over; engine overhauls would cost $30,000 on the Baron while the Beech 18's big, round radial engines could be had for $2,500. They burned more gas but at twenty-five cents a gallon, he could afford $15 an hour.

---

[4] Russ Clanton's Phillips Station

"Besides," he paused, considering the effects of an engine failure, "the Beech 18 can run all day on one engine, and it has a larger, more comfortable cabin."

As his businesses grew, David bought more airplanes. His next purchase was a Rockwell Turbo Commander. He leased it to Med Express in Show Low, Arizona, and flew it for them. Then he bought a Learjet because he'd always wanted to fly a jet. With a charter company managing the Lear as an air ambulance, David served as co-pilot to transport patients to and from MD Anderson Cancer Center in Houston.

On our first visit to David's place, we had learned the complex which awed us as we taxied after landing was called Texas Sports Ranch, a business David built to support competition gymnastics. That long and substantial main building had four hundred dormitory-style beds, two full gymnastics arenas, an indoor soccer court, and a full athletic camp-style kitchen. Outside were four football and soccer fields, as well as a Junior Olympic pool.

He had hosted church and cheerleading camps, as well as leadership and team-building retreats. Once, while hosting a national gym meet, David was approached by airshow celebrity Bobby Younkin, who wanted to buy the Learjet to use in an airshow routine. Bobby's daughter was competing in the meet. She would become the lovely Amanda Younkin Franklin, a top airshow wing walker until a tragic accident took her life in 2011 — and the entire aviation community mourned.

Linda: David told us that we could always find him on Saturday mornings having breakfast with other area pilots at a regular gathering place. He invited us to join him. We discovered it was kind of like the one described in Bob Jamison's book,

Airplanes, Alligators, and Hi-Fin Blues. I love that book of stories that came out of a regular gathering of aviators and friends.

In the first chapter, Bob tells a story about a flight to Belize where the guys were going fishing. Bob had snuck a nine-foot boa constrictor onto David's Beech 18 because he promised a friend who had smuggled it out that he'd return it to its home country. The boa wouldn't eat in captivity. Bob neglected to mention the snake to David until they were walking across the ramp to the Belize airport terminal.

Customs officials were startled by the illicit cargo stuffed in a burlap sack. David, just learning he'd had a fourth passenger across the Gulf of Mexico, didn't appreciate Bob's desire to help a friend. He thought for sure they'd throw Bob in jail, but Bob shrugged it off, convincing nervous customs workers they'd have to confiscate it. For years after that, Bob and his cohorts back home in Dayton, Texas, had a good laugh at their Saturday morning breakfasts.

David flew his Beech 18 all over the U.S. and Central America. He used to fly to Mexico, until drug smuggling became rampant. He worried that smugglers would steal his airplane—perfect for such clandestine trips.

Mike: Full restoration took a few more years. Then David's beloved and well-traveled Beech 18, the one that carried Bob Jamison and friends to Belize, winged her way to a new home at the Beechcraft Heritage Museum in Tullahoma, Tennessee. Only this time, without a boa on board.

M & M Air Service

Mike: The proclamation came from George Mitchell, second-generation manager and president of family-owned and -operated M & M Air Service. "April 9th, 1946! That's the day aerial seeding of rice fields in Southeast Texas began, and it has been here ever since!"

The company was founded in Beaumont on that date by Poley and Fields Mitchell and Gilbert Mapes. They bid on two hundred government-surplus Stearmans and were awarded forty-two, for $56.56 each. They reconfigured most of those airplanes for aerial application of wet and dry materials.

Poley and Fields purchased Gilbert's share of the business a year later. Through M & M, generations of Mitchells have continually served the farming communities here.

When M & M began, there were 150,000 acres of rice production to cover. Their airplanes took to the air before sunrise, working the fields until well after dark. For twenty years, M & M used up to thirty-three Stearmans within the tri-county area.

A Stearman can haul about 1,400 pounds, but it's pretty slow. Valuable time was wasted waiting for them to fly back to reload. To solve this problem, each farm made room for an airstrip. M & M's loaders and ground handlers refilled the airplanes' hoppers with chemicals on site.

According to George, there were 172 airstrips on farms in the three counties. "We called them Stearman strips because the Stearmans didn't require that much runway to get airborne. One day, Henry Morrison and I were each flying a Stearman and broke the record for the number of loads flown in one day: 197 loads."

For twenty years, rice was 100 percent of M & M's revenue. When the area's rice production dropped to 25,000 acres, M & M had to change with the times. Diversification was the key to survival. Their contracts now include aerial firefighting in West Texas, crop dusting in Southeast Texas and the Midwest, and fertilizing timber throughout several southern states. M & M's customers have included the U.S. Department of the Interior, the Texas Forest Service, the Bureau of Indian Affairs, and the Bureau of Land Management. They've also sprayed local area counties for mosquitoes after hurricanes and reseeded burned areas for the U.S. Forest Service. These days, spraying rice may only account for 8 percent of the business.

They also no longer use Stearmans for spraying. They've been replaced by Air Tractors, manufactured in Olney, Texas. According to George, "Since 1946, the price of airplanes has multiplied by ten thousand. The last airplane we purchased was $565,000."

But technology has advanced significantly. Workers no longer stand at the ends of rows in the fields, waving flags to show crop dusting pilots where to turn.

David Mitchell, vice president and third generation at M & M Air Service, remembered, "When I was a kid, we were happy if all we had to flag was a thousand acres in a day. We got up early, climbed across ditches and fences, flagging our way across muddy rice fields, working late into the evenings. With today's technology, GPS, and electronics, there are no flaggers. It's safer."

Better education has improved safety, too. Ag pilots receive considerable training and continuing education—a minimum of twenty units in the areas of pesticides and chemical applications every three years. Annual safety meetings and daily briefings are additional requirements, and taking special courses offered at conventions earns insurance discounts.

These days, pilots plot latitude and longitudinal waypoints to create electronic shape files of fields. They load the files directly into the airplane's onboard computer system. With the programming ability to exclude an area from spraying, the pilot creates a flight plan. They may fly a racetrack pattern or parallel rows as they did when flaggers were employed. A data logger tracks the plane's actual flight, heading, and altitude. Once that information is downloaded, it becomes a permanent record of what was sprayed.

All this new technology that brought changes to crop dusting required a major adjustment for older pilots. Mark Mitchell gave an example. "One of our pilots flew almost exclusively in Liberty County for forty-three years, but when we used GPS and data loggers in 1993, that was it for him. After thirty-thousand-plus hours of aerial application, the system retired him."

With such history, nostalgia is unavoidable. On a trip through Hartsville, South Carolina, David Mitchell met a pilot who said, "Are you from M & M? You gotta see this." He opened the hangar doors, and there was one of their old Stearmans, beautifully restored.

Another was found working fields in Sumter, South Carolina. Their number 21 Stearman, the first airplane in Texas to sow rice by air, is in the Chambers County Agricultural Historical Museum in Winnie. Their number 34 Stearman was donated to the National Agricultural Aviation Museum in Jackson, Mississippi.

The last Stearman in the M & M stable was used for training until it suffered heavy damage from Hurricane Ike. Since being restored, the Mitchell family of pilots has flown it occasionally as part of their history, but it's retired from the heavy work.

Not that anyone needs evidence of the Mitchells' decades of contributions, but one can find the proof in museums and hangars, rescued and renewed, that appropriately honors their lifelong dedication to the community.

Born to Fly

Deftly they opened the brain of a child,
and it was full of flying dreams.

—Stanley Kunitz, *My Surgeons*

Lauren Jones, Young Aviatrix

When we first met her, Lauren Jones did not strike us as your average ten-year-old, and not just because her birthday was on February 29, Leap Day. It was a maturity beyond her years and a real love for people and flying. Her passion for aviation may have been encouraged even before her first flight in her father's Beechcraft Bonanza at the age of two weeks.

Stephen Jones was working out of town when his wife, Christine, went into labor, signaling an early arrival of little Lauren, their first child. He took off from Baton Rouge in his Bonanza, hurrying home to Dry Creek, a residential airpark west of Houston. He hoped to arrive in time to take Christine to the hospital.

His former flight instructor was also flying that morning and happened to be on the same radio frequency. Surprised to hear his instructor's voice after many years, Stephen blurted over the airwaves, "Mama's having a baby!"

Approaching the Houston area, the air traffic controller cleared him direct through Bush Intercontinental airspace and over the top of the busy commercial airport. As this was an unusual clearance, he surmised the controller must have heard him state his mission.

Lauren has heard the story of her birth many times. "It was a good thing, because I might not have made it if Daddy hadn't come back in time. He took my mom to the hospital, and when I came out, I wasn't breathing." The hospital staff got Lauren breathing and took her to Texas Children's Hospital, where she checked out okay.

Baby Lauren, 8 months old

Our introduction to Lauren and her dad came during a Valentine's Day flying treasure hunt that concluded in Lufkin. Visiting with her in the restaurant at the Angelina County Airport was more like conversing with an adult. Lauren is an easy person to be around—she's intelligent, articulate, enthusiastic, friendly, and compassionate. We could quickly forget she was so young.

A couple months later at a Young Eagles Day at Pearland Regional Airport, while Stephen was taking kids for rides in his Bonanza, Lauren helped with ground school, registration, and welcoming visitors. She took a break to talk with us about her passion. The sign of a true aviator soul, she gets pumped sharing the experience of flight.

"I like taking my friends flying," she began. "We take them sightseeing, like around the San Jacinto Monument, to Brenham for lunch, and seeing all the beautiful lights of downtown Houston at night. I prefer flying. It's just the way we travel." Her favorite part is the takeoff because, as she said with contagious excitement, "It means we're up, and free!"

We wondered about her earliest memories of life aloft. Since she didn't have very far back to reflect, her recollections were clear. By the time she was four and just out of her car seat, she was learning to navigate, knew how to look for airport beacons at night, and was racking up right-seat time.

About the age most kids are learning to read, Lauren was learning runway orientation and airport traffic patterns. "It's pretty easy. Just follow the road and look for certain landmarks. Turning final coming home to Dry Creek is where you turn over Walmart—of course, that depends on if you're landing on One Eight or Three Six—it was base the other day, so that means we were landing on One Eight."

Of course, the grownups at Dry Creek have had fun with her on the radio. "Dad will do touch-and-goes, and some of our neighbors get on the radio and say, 'Great touch-and-go, Lauren! That's a ten! Are you going to let your dad do one now?'" She laughed adorably. "My feet don't even reach the rudder pedals yet, so I wasn't really landing it."

As aviators do, Lauren's had adventures, like flying to Galveston, and to AirVenture in Oshkosh for the world's largest aviation convention. "It was really busy flying into Oshkosh, but it was fun! With four airplanes landing in front of us and three behind, you have to land and get out of the way.

"One time we flew to Galveston and got a ride from the airport to Moody Gardens. But when we were ready to come back to the airport, we couldn't find a ride. A fancy charter bus came by, and Dad asked if we could get a lift to the airport. The driver said, 'Sure,' and let us in because it was empty. As we were stepping off the bus, Dad tipped him, and the driver said, 'Thanks! Now, I have to get going. There's a bride and groom waiting on me!'"

Lauren remembered that *oops!* moment: "I imagined a couple dressed in wedding attire for their important day, waiting as we unknowingly detoured their ride."

Lauren brings out the best in people and is at ease with older folks as much as those her age. One of the Jones's neighbors was a retired airline pilot and U.S. Air Force colonel, the late Gale Haskins, who had a Stearman and a PT-19. Gale and several other neighbors joined forces to fly the Missing Man formation over Lauren's school on Veteran's Day.

In this symbolic tradition, four airplanes fly in a V-shaped formation. Then one pulls up in a vertical climb, leaving the position and creating an empty space as the rest continue their course. Often flown over memorial services and veteran events, the Missing Man honors members of the armed forces our country has lost in battle. No wonder Lauren was so proud of her fly-in community and especially fond of Colonel Haskins.

Her bright smile beams out of her whole being and her eyes sparkle when she speaks of friends and aviation, and in particular of Gale Haskins. "Colonel Haskins was a hurricane hunter and had lots of cool stuff in his hangar. I really liked him; he influenced my flying a lot."

She rode with him in both his airplanes but loved the Stearman best. "When he took me flying the first time, he asked if I had bugs in my teeth. I said no, so he asked, 'You're not smiling?' I told him I was smiling, but thankfully there was a windshield keeping the bugs from getting in my teeth."

As they taxied back over the creek to his hangar, Colonel Haskins asked Lauren if she had brought her fishing pole, to which she replied deftly and with quick wit, "You really should keep some spares in here. Then you could just throw out your rod and drag it in the creek as you taxi by." And, she had sympathy for him when they had to move the mailboxes so the Stearman's lower wing wouldn't hit them as he taxied across the bridge over the not-so-dry creek to his hangar.

Dry Creek residents share responsibilities of maintaining their airpark, and before Lauren came along the volunteers were all adults. But she changed that.

"I'm on the Nominating Committee. I go to all the airport meetings, and when they asked for volunteers for the committee, I raised my hand. At first, all the adults laughed, but I just kept my hand up, and soon they stopped laughing." Lauren convinced them she was the one who could match people with the right jobs, such as taking care of that creek.

Could there be anything about flying that's not just perfect for her? Well, yes. Flying over damage from Hurricane Katrina made her sad. But closer to home, when Lauren and her dad went flying, her little sister Amy usually didn't join them. During the Young Eagles day in Pearland, Amy opted to attend a birthday party while Lauren declined invitations to two birthday parties with her best friends in favor of working at the fly-in.

"We have so much fun, and I always wish she was with us," Lauren sweetly lamented. But she understood Amy had different interests, and maybe a bit of anxiety about flying. So, on those few occasions when Amy did ride along, Lauren sat in the back with her, holding her hand and helping calm her fears. "Like the time when we flew to Little Rock to see our grandparents at Christmas, and we had a little turbulence. All the boxes of Christmas presents stacked behind us toppled over on us."

Bumpy air is the kind of stuff Lauren takes in stride because it's part of flying. "Another time we had turbulence and it was kind of like being on a roller coaster. When we dropped down, everything came flying up—even the dirt we had tracked in when we got in the airplane!"

In contemplative pause, she looked out the hangar past the picnic tables and chairs, the grill with hot dogs and hamburgers, and parents waiting for eager kids on their first flight and gazed at her family's Bonanza. Her dad was loading another child for a Young Eagles flight.

With a nod toward their plane, she said, "You know, our Bonanza hasn't always looked like this. They rebuilt the engine when I was in kindergarten." With that statement her tone seemed a little melancholy, but it wasn't immediately apparent why. Surely the new engine was a good thing, so why the somberness?

She continued before we could ask. "When the new engine came, that was a big day for me, because you know, in kindergarten you don't have homework so I could be around to watch."

She could even engage Amy in the fun by playing in a box with Styrofoam peanuts. And being near her father has always been a significant part of what draws her. "Dad built a cubicle in the hangar for me so I could sit there and draw and be close to him while he put in the engine."

However, the engine was not the only upgrade. Next, they installed a fresh interior. As she talked, her disappointment was clear. "The seats and interior were already nice, but I guess they needed to be replaced." She paused in memory. "It was down for *three months*! That was hard on me."

The only thing left to change on the Jones family's Bonanza was the paint. Lauren had kept her hopes up that they would not make any further changes to the airplane she was used to. "I really liked it the way it was. It was orange and brown. I could tell it looked like the seventies because I've seen stuff from the seventies."

An air traffic controller liked it, too. At least someone sided with her. "He said it reminded him of when he was learning to fly."

Lauren and the controller were outvoted and she cried when the airplane was taken to the paint shop. "I knew there was no way I could change their minds." Resigned to the loss, she took pictures as keepsakes of the old familiar paint scheme she loved.

All that time she and her airplane were separated, Lauren struggled, missing her beloved Bonanza. "I needed comforting," she explained, "so I went flying with our neighbor, Mr. Henry, in his Bonanza."

The airplane has undergone many changes since Lauren was in kindergarten. "Like the wingtips. Dad bought them in an online auction. He let me stay up late to watch the bidding because someone else was bidding against us. He really wanted those wingtips. Finally, he just put in a high amount. I guess the other person gave up." She smiled proudly and expounded. "The new tips make the airplane lighter so it can carry a little more weight."

The wingtips, it seemed, were the only uplifting modification. The rest, well, we can understand why she grappled with the changes to the airplane she treasured. Yet, at the same time, she was so mature.

At the time we met her, Lauren already had plans for college. That is, she hoped her dad would have another airplane so that she could have the Bonanza. She articulated her reason convincingly. "It's the airplane I've flown in all my life, and it's very special to me." Then she offered diplomatically, "But I know it's special to Dad, too. And he's used to it. So I might have to be the one to have a new airplane because he might have a hard time parting with it."

The years have passed since that day we first met Lauren. Before she started college at Baylor University to study aviation sciences, she learned the answer to her question. She would be the one to get a new airplane. Learning to fly in her Cardinal 177RG meant her dad wouldn't have to part with the Bonanza after all.

Lauren Jones, 2019

Jed Keck: A Lucky Guy

Linda: Years ago, in Dayton, Texas, young Jed Keck dreamed of flying. While riding in the family car, his eyes widened and fixed upon the agricultural spray planes along Highway 90 on the way to Beaumont. Sometimes the drive was perfectly synchronized with airplanes taking off or landing. Catching those moments made Jed feel lucky.

But learning about airplanes was a challenge. Aviation books and magazines were scarce in his town. "The Dayton Elementary School library had exactly two books on aviation, and I cannot tell you how many times I looked through them," he recalled. "One was *Ann Can Fly,* about a girl and her father flying in his new Cessna floatplane. The other was a reference book with a lot of pictures."

So he searched for anything having to do with aviation, always thirsting for more. He found a book of aviation stories at the drugstore on Dayton's Main Street and cut airplane pictures from newspapers and magazines. At one point, he had collected over two hundred airplane pictures and taped them to his bedroom wall. He no longer has the pictures, but he does have the drugstore book.

"Around here," he noted, "most things that flew were ag planes and buzzards." With so few opportunities to know more about flying, when the Civil Air Patrol (CAP) formed a cadet squadron in neighboring Liberty, Jed's dream came a little closer to reality.

Their squadron scheduled a field trip to Ellington Air Force Base, which was quite busy during those Vietnam War days. Cadets were to be at Ellington Saturday morning. "I was the only kid who showed up." He still shrugs in disbelief.

"The big deal for me was getting a ride in the CAP's T-34, which had flown over from its home base at the Liberty airport. This was my first time to fly and for a twelve-year-old, that T-34 with its military paint scheme was a major warbird." Since Jed was the only kid there, he got the whole hour of flight.

Mike: He speaks fondly of the Liberty airport, remembering bits and pieces of the people and airplanes that left an impression on him, like the blue-and-white Stearman of Liberty Air Service, a pilot from M & M Air Service who wore a beat-up white helmet with air holes drilled in it—an unusual sight since most weren't wearing helmets back then—and a lady's airplane he washed and waxed so she could race it in the Powder Puff Derby.

As a teen, he immersed himself further in aviation by working for local rice farmers as a flagger for the ag pilots who would dump rows of seeds or dust their fields with herbicides. Jed and other boys held position flags to let the crop dusters know when they were at the end of a row—in a way, the human predecessor to GPS. The job gave him a chance to learn more about the ag planes and their colorful pilots.

Often while working in those rice fields, elder and fellow Daytonite Bob Jamison flew low overhead in his Citabria, buzzing around the combines and auger carts. Jed never rode in the Citabria, but he was always thrilled to see it.

Bob would have appreciated Jed's fond memories, as he had also flagged in those fields when he was a teen. Now he was just having fun in his little plane. Bob didn't know it then, but his jaunts over the rice fields added encouragement for a future world-class pilot.

How That Little Kid from Dayton Became a Globe-Trotting Pilot

After his first airplane ride with the Civil Air Patrol, Jed didn't immediately have more opportunities to fly. But in 1975, Richard Human joined the Dayton school district to teach drafting classes, and the best part was that Mr. Human was a pilot.

In a little shed behind his house, he built a single-seat Volksplane. Using Jed's pickup truck, he towed the fuselage out to the airport. Then, in a mentoring move Jed will never forget, Mr. Human paid Jed for the tow with a ride in his Piper Cub, arguably the epitome of general aviation.

Jed returned to the Liberty airport in June 1978 to take the first five lessons toward his private pilot certificate. The instructor's signature is no longer legible in his logbook, but Jed recalled that he lived east of Liberty in a house with a grass strip behind it. The first time he saw the man's home, there was a Cessna 182 parked out front. Jed thought, *Now,* this *is living.*

When the instructor left to fly for Eastern Airlines, Jed continued his lessons at Beaumont Municipal Airport where he worked with aviation writer and Southeast Texas radio host

Gordon Baxter. On New Year's Eve 1979, Jed became a real pilot at the Jefferson County Airport in Port Arthur. That led to a job as a line boy and mechanic's helper at Bristow Helicopters in Sabine Pass.

After some experience, he earned an airframe and powerplant mechanic certificate at SOWELA Tech in Lake Charles.[5] Working as an airplane mechanic, Jed could afford to fly more, adding ratings to his pilot certificate.

While most of his early flying was more the "bush" type—that is, backcountry flying into short, rugged landing strips off the edge of the map, places far away from the civilized world—he is airline transport rated in airplanes, multi-engine land and sea, and helicopters. He also holds jet type ratings, and inspector authorization as an aircraft mechanic.

Now years later, that little boy from Dayton who once dreamed of flying has flown on every continent and in about half the countries of the world. He has captured and tagged wildlife, flown live-line power line maintenance from a helicopter, delivered firearms to mercenaries, flown corporate jets, and more.

When a flight department in the Seattle area contacted Jed, it turned out to be a job offer from Microsoft co-founder Paul Allen. Jed was hired to fly helicopters and a Twin Otter on amphibious floats. He flew the boss's helicopters from yachts around the world, providing security for the owners and guests.

---

[5] Southwest Louisiana Technical Community College.

Finding the Evangel

Linda: One of the places his flying career has taken him was the island of Yap in the Western Pacific. It was there in 2007 that he spotted a piece of history, a rare airplane Jed had only read about.

From the late 1960s to the early 1970s, Carl Mortensen of Orange City, Iowa, designed the Evangel 4500 twin-engine bush plane. He built eight of them and captured the interest of *Air Progress Magazine* for a feature article in 1974. Jed had even met Carl in 1995, but up until this time he had never seen an Evangel in person. Now, here was one parked in a corner of the airport. It looked really rough.

Recognizing his find, he inquired at a nearby hangar. The hangar belonged to Pacific Missionary Aviation. PMA flew to the Micronesian Islands where no one else would fly.

With little time to examine the plane, PMA pilots gave him the short story.[6] Their missionary founder, Ed Kalau, had flown this Evangel from Iowa to Yap eastbound over the Atlantic, Europe, and Asia in 1974. He retired the airplane in 1994 and sold it, but the new owner never transferred the registration.

After returning from his short stay on Yap, Jed called the pilots and told them he wanted to salvage the plane. He had the relic deemed legally abandoned and offered one dollar, promising to have it removed by the end of the year.

While back in the States, Jed looked up Carl Mortensen. They spent the day together and talked about the best process

---

[6] The PMA pilots were Peter Richert and Vince Davis.

for taking the Evangel apart. Then Carl mentioned that Ed Kalau was living in Guam and encouraged Jed to stop there on his way back to Yap for the plane.

Ed was a World War II Luftwaffe fighter pilot. He had been shot down and taken prisoner by the British. He was a former Nazi turned Christian missionary who had become a U.S. citizen. He shared photos of the Evangel serial number 006 when it was new and stories of its history. At least four people were born in that plane, he said. The Evangel Jed had just bought for a dollar was the very plane in that feature article he read in *Air Progress Magazine*.

After their visit, Jed left Guam and continued on to Yap where a pleasant surprise awaited. PMA pilots had located all the paperwork—logbooks, tags, letters, and brochures. It would be helpful in the restoration and valuable in telling the airplane's story.

Over the next nine days, the good folks of PMA disassembled the plane, loaded it into a container, and shipped it to the States for restoration. The one-dollar purchase would still be expensive to restore; just shipping it to the U.S. cost a pretty penny.

The Evangel left Yap in January 2008. Held up by customs in Hong Kong, Shanghai, and Hawaii, it finally arrived in Seattle in May. After long and careful consideration about the best way to preserve this piece of aviation history, Jed donated the Evangel to the Iowa Aviation Museum with the hope that it will fly again.

Restoration depends on funds, and who knows how long it will take. But in the end, it will tell a good story, including Jed's part in its rescue.

A Lucky Guy

The Evangel also encouraged Jed to think about his retirement years—maybe a hangar at an airport where he'd rebuild airplanes. But that would require him to leave his house and drive to work. He cringed at the thought. A house on an airpark was appealing, but owning an entire airstrip had even more appeal.

In searching for an established public airstrip for sale, most of what Jed found was out of his price range or in the wrong location. A fully public airstrip would bring headaches he did not want. What he really wanted was a grass airstrip to dedicate for use by antique, vintage, and classic aircraft. Private, yet open for use by permission.

To have open-cockpit airplanes around as much as possible, climate and location relative to a large metro area would be of primary importance. The property's shape and flatness would also be crucial for an airstrip.

After an exhaustive search, Jed found the forty-acre site next to Old Fort Parker. This was once the home of the Parker family, now a place of Texas and Indian history. There was only a small log home on a hayfield. Limestone County and the towns of Groesbeck and Mexia had acquired the property from the state, including a two-thousand-foot strip of grass with the possibility of expansion.

He pitched his idea to stakeholders for based airplanes and occasional fly-ins. The local leaders were enthusiastic about the economic benefits and appeal to the community, and the FAA gave the project its blessing.

Fly-ins at Fort Parker Flying Field quickly became popular summertime destinations, especially on second Saturdays when there's ice cream for all. This is where Jed Keck feels at home. Like a part of his childhood all over again, when the drive was perfectly synchronized with airplanes taking off or landing and catching those moments made him feel lucky.

The Ace

Linda: A boy named Jim filled his glass jar with gasoline, hopped back on his bike, lawn mower in tow, and pedaled out in search of tall grassy yards. Gas was twenty-five cents per gallon. An enterprising young man could make money if he was willing to look and work for it.

The filling station owner had noticed the youngster and offered him a job. Jim had long admired the men who stood at the station's pump island with their pressed uniforms, tire gauges in their shirt pockets, and smiling faces. He accepted the job thinking of the respect he would earn when he quickly serviced cars belonging to ladies like his mother who stopped in for gas.

Jim worked his way up from cleaning hubcaps, vacuuming floors, and washing windows. He wore his crisp uniform proudly as he stood at the pump island like a sentinel surveying his domain.

One Sunday morning, his grandfather drove past on his way home from church. An Austrian prisoner of war captured during World War I, Jim's grandfather had been held in Crosby, Texas. After the war, he saw opportunities here that were not available in Austria and declined the free trip back to Europe to become a U.S. citizen.

Grandfather glanced at his grandson sternly, driving on without waving back. Later that evening, young Jim would learn an important life lesson.

Grandfather: "Vat ver you doing, and vy ver you not in church dis morning?"

Jim: "Well, that's my shift."

No matter what image he thought he'd built for himself, Jim's grandfather encouraged him to do better by God's standards. "Come to my shop, undt you can vork every day after school undt not miss church on Sunday."

Although the new job didn't have the same prestige, this place full of machines was fascinating. Jim started at the bottom, pushing a broom. Soon the other men working there showed him how to run the machines, entrusting him with work—although the customers weren't convinced yet of the kid's abilities.

When the men left on vacation or hunting trips and customer orders stacked up, Jim decided he would fill them on his own. He taught himself to type so he could create invoices as though he had turned the work over to the machinists. The customers never knew differently, and Jim kept quiet about it. Before long, he was a journeyman machinist. Understanding mechanics also helped him as a pilot.

Jim learned to fly at a young age. His father was an airplane mechanic. His mom would drop him off at the airport after school, and he'd climb the fence, pull a friend's Piper Cub out of a hangar, and go flying. Then he'd fill it up and push it back in the hangar. He was hooked on flying, and for a few short years after earning his private pilot certificate, he took to the air every chance he had.

Mike: But Jim was also called to serve our country. He thought he would be an aircraft mechanic, like his dad, only he would get to work on turbine engines in the Air Force. That's what his scores on the military's aptitude tests indicated—he was a natural in mechanical things.

His second-highest score was in electrical, but he hoped they wouldn't rely on him for that. He feared his color confusion might cause him to connect wires wrong. He'd had enough confirmation as a child to know that would not go well. Whenever another kid pulled the labels off a crayon, he was just as happy coloring the trees blue and the sky green, because he couldn't see the difference.

The fact that he would get a free education made him excited about his future. But that didn't last long.

The new cadets must have been lined up nine million deep, he estimated, to find out where Uncle Sam was going to send them. Sergeants came by and pulled every seventh or eighth guy out of line, including Jim. When he learned his fate, he was dumbfounded. Medic school? The only answer he received was that they needed medics more than they needed mechanics. In Vietnam, guys were getting shot. They would teach him what he needed to know.

During training in Wichita Falls, all the soon-to-be medics practiced on each other, as evidence by the hundreds of bruised arms, lessons on finding a vein. Jim felt like a pincushion.

The next phase, observing procedures, made him queasy. "The medic told a patient to take a breath; it might hurt. Then he poked this long needle into the guy's side and worked it in deep. I thought I'd better take a breath, too."

Inside that long pneumatic needle was a thin rod with a barbed claw on the end. When the rod stopped (against something), the medic gave the needle a quick push to shove those barbs in, then pulled out a piece of meat. Jim had just witnessed a liver biopsy.

"They put a Band-Aid over the hole and told him he'd be fine. I thought, *Wait 'til the pain meds wear off.* Jim felt faint until a nurse asked him, "You ever hunt and fish? Ever skin a deer?" He had, but the animals were dead. She pointed to another patient whose wounds were more serious, and in an effort to help, she said, "That guy over there on the gurney is conked out. He can't feel this, and we are fixing him."

From then on, Jim was able to handle the gory job of a military medic during wartime. Holding sponges and sopping fluids, surgery became like mechanics, and the pneumatic shot became a fun tool to scare new recruits. He liked splitting a phone book in half, pretending to test the calibration as they stood in line for shots.

After a while, Jim rode in the back of C-130s bringing in busloads of wounded soldiers. They could load three hundred stretchers on the plane. On every flight, he made rounds, checking IVs, administering pain killers, and encouraging the men. From his service as a medic, Jim earned credentials as a physician's assistant. He gave it his best, but it wasn't his calling.

These days, when he has an occasion to walk into a clinic or doctor's office, he wonders only momentarily what his life would be like if he had pursued the career the Air Force handed him. Then he thinks of the path he chose, remembering how he couldn't wait to get back to the shop and the craftsmanship of making something out of a lump of steel. It was more fun grinding metal on a lathe or beating on stuff with a chisel. He has no regrets.

He also returned to flying after the service. His Maule M-5 and a Cessna 185 have been perfect for airpark living, for landing at his ranch in West Texas, and for camping in the north forty at Oshkosh.

The idiom "holding court" best describes what happens when Jim Kubik comes to Saturday morning breakfast gatherings of aviators in Baytown, which is most of the time. Ever the entertainer, although long past the phonebook-splitting trick, he always seems to have plenty of philosophizing to do. Kind of the Mike Rowe of pilots, with a West Texas accent.

Influenced by the character and faith of his grandfather, his dad, and others who have mentored him, Jim has become a leader in his church and community. He isn't afraid to treat people with kindness and respect, nor will he apologize for what he believes in. Alongside the sign that reads "Ace Machine Shop" on his massive building is a cross and the words, "Jesus is the answer."

The Life o' Riley

Mike: For four months out of the year, Coda Riley works from sunrise to sunset every day. It's a grueling schedule for a grueling job, and he loves it.

He's certified as a firefighting Level 2 SEAT pilot (Single Engine Air Tanker) and has worked as an ag pilot for years. When crop dusting, he estimates he makes about seventy takeoffs and landings a day and turns around over the fields he's spraying about two thousand times. That takes a lot of arm muscle.

Since earning his commercial certificate, he's also worked as a corporate pilot, towed banners over Houston skies on weekends, ferried airplanes, dropped skydivers, and towed and piloted gliders. He even appeared in *Animal Planet's* "River Monsters" when he flew the show's host, Jeremy Wade, around the Baytown area while filming.

A pretty tough guy who's as down-to-earth as they come, Coda has developed outstanding skill as an aviator and enjoys sharing his love of flight. He took a break from professional aviating to pilot his Cessna 170B to the fly-in camp-out adventure at Critters Lodge, a grass strip near Centerville, Texas.

Walking up to the large hangar where appreciative, happy lodge guests were devouring food, Coda took a seat and joined in the conversation. But sitting doesn't hold his attention for long. He looked for someone who might be interested in an airplane ride. "I go to fly-ins to fly, not sit!"

It wasn't long until he started up his engine and taxied out to enjoy the perfect weather. The air molecules would behave at his command, providing lift to his high-wing taildragger, propelling him through the atmosphere, an open playground for the pilot. Everyone admired his aerial demonstration and low passes down the turf strip.

Linda: I watched with envy. It had been a while since I learned to fly a tailwheel airplane. There wasn't much wind the day I received my tailwheel endorsement, but I was required to prove I could land it in a crosswind. Therefore, I used the alternate method: fast taxi (without taking off) on just one main wheel. With the plane tilted to the side, this demonstrates the pilot's ability to maintain control when landing with wind from the right or left. Having been through that training, I knew when I saw Coda land and keep the airplane on one wheel that he was in control of his plane.

"Flying," he says, "is like a cat. A cat just picks you. You don't own a cat; a cat owns you. Flying is like that. It owns you."

It picked him when he was two years old. His parents were driving to their new house in the country when he saw a crop duster. "I heard the noise, then I saw it. They were flying on the deck. In that moment, I knew what I wanted."

Coda grew up mostly in Fannett, Texas, one of three boys who were encouraged to play outside to discover the world around them. This strapping young man could have played any sport easily. But nobody in his family was a pilot nor wanted him to fly, so he had to figure out on his own how one becomes a pilot. About ten years after his first glimpse of a crop duster, his family was driving through Port Neches for a church event when they passed a house where a man was working on a small airplane (an ultralight) in the yard. Glued to the truck window, Coda would remember that house.

A few years later, his father bought a new home just two blocks from where he'd seen the ultralight. Coda walked over to the house and waited, eager to meet the man with the airplane. Finally, a truck pulled up, and Coda caught the man between the truck and front door.

"Hi, my name's Coda, and I'm an airplane nut!"

The man turned and looked at him funny. "What?"

Coda feared he had blown his opportunity, but he repeated himself. "My name's Coda, and I'm an airplane nut!"

The man chuckled. "Oh, well my name's Charlie. Come on in."

"Doc" Charlie Smith took Coda to his garage and showed him his full-size airplane and the ultralight. Then he invited him in to meet his wife. Doc and Coda talked at length about aviation, and instantly, Coda felt like he'd finally met his best friend.

"There's a fly-in at Pleasure Island next weekend. Would you like to go?" Doc asked.

There was nothing Coda wanted more. Now fifteen years after the toddler was awed by a crop duster, he would finally get to ride in an airplane. An eager neophyte enthralled with flying will cause an instructor to want to share more experiences. On the way to the fly-in, Doc let Coda fly, just to get the feel of it, because watching the teenager at the controls made Doc just as happy as Coda.

There was all kinds of fun at the fly-in: food, airplanes, and a host of other airplane nuts just like Coda. There was even a balloon-popping competition. People stood along the runway and released helium-filled balloons. The object of the game was for pilots to chase the balloons in flight and burst them with their airplane's propeller. The contestant who destroyed the most would win.

Doc asked Coda if he would like to give it a try. The pair hopped back in Doc's airplane and launched for their turn in the contest. Coda nailed the first balloon. *Pop!* Then they came back around, and Coda whacked the second balloon. Then, the third and fourth. *Pop! Pop! Pop!* He won second place in the contest, despite never having flown before that day. The following week, Doc gave him his first real flight lesson. He said Coda was the most natural pilot he'd ever met, and after the second lesson—just two hours of flight training—Doc signed him off for his first solo flight.

When they weren't flying, they worked on airplanes or just hung out together. The admiration and respect were mutual. Doc was his hero. He had been an instructor pilot during World War II, shot down two Japanese Zeroes, and had flown more than two hundred missions over Burma and China. There was so much to learn from Doc, and Coda soaked up every opportunity.

When Doc received a package from the Chinese government containing the Distinguished Flying Cross, Coda was there when he opened it. That moment is one he will always treasure, one that he carries with him on those hot, grueling days from sunup to sundown, in some of the highest-risk non-combat flying that exists.

Mike: All flying requires vigilance, but more so with crop dusters. They say if a crop duster hasn't hit a wire yet, the pilot isn't flying low enough. And if the pilot isn't low enough, that's grounds for termination. Coda once hit three power lines in one swoop. Sliced them right up.

The lower wire was chopped in half by the prop. The other two slid over the plane, shearing off the tail. Usually, if you see them, you center punch them. Boom! He never saw them, but he sure felt the impact. Coda pulled up and circled. The plane felt normal. Then he landed, and sure enough, there was evidence of wires. It cost $120,000 for an engine teardown and prop overhaul.

He also developed a busy aircraft ferrying business that has birthed some interesting events, like the time the prop came off over Stigler, Oklahoma. Of that incident, he says unassumingly, "I made an uneventful landing in a doctor's hay meadow."

But then there was the summer of 2018, when he was taking off from a small town in Minnesota in a Turbine Thrush, and the engine quit on takeoff. He hit his emergency dump to free the chemicals on board and prepared for an off-airport landing. The airplane came down violently in a seven-foot-tall corn patch and flipped over. That corn had just snatched him right out of the air. Strapped in by the seatbelt and shoulder harness, Coda hung upside down, chemical residue seeping into his eyes, nose, and lungs. There were 200 gallons of jet fuel in both wing tanks.

The top of the cockpit had been crushed in. Coda couldn't get the doors open. He beat on them, tearing the skin on his elbows. Finally, he popped his seatbelt loose and, standing in the upside-down cabin, kicked the doors open and crawled out through the corn patch.

The stalks were so tall, Coda couldn't see the road. Although he was shaken, he knew to walk in the direction of the nose. He came upon the engine twenty feet from the airplane. Despite his back hurting between the shoulder blades and chemical burns, he made it to the road. Just then, the farmer's wife came running, relieved to see him. She let him inside to shower off the chemicals. Coda washed and rinsed ten times before going to the hospital for a checkout.

At the hospital, the staff worried he might endanger other patients, so they made him stay outside in the parking lot and called the fire department. Emergency responders set up freestanding curtains around Coda and instructed him to strip down. They brought their detox kit, but they couldn't figure out how it worked. Without experience in detoxification but dead set on protocol, responders sprayed him with cold water from a fire hose, as he shivered behind the curtains buck naked.

Linda: Coda knows that if you get bumped off the horse, you'd better get right back on it. Nurses assumed he would want some pain medication, but Coda said no, because he was going to fly. Back at the airport, he pulled his plane, an RV-4, out of the hangar and took off. In his own way, this fighter won with a K.O. to the accident by doing barrel rolls and loops over his crash site.

With no agricultural spray plane to fly, Coda was essentially without a job. But only for a moment. He wasn't even up in his RV-4 ten minutes when he received a text from an ag operator in Kansas in urgent need of a crop duster. Coda was at work by 10:00 a.m. the next day.

Given his experience and determination, we weren't surprised when he beat us by a quarter inch in a spot landing contest at Debby Rihn-Harvey's fly-in at the La Porte airport. In fact, we were darn proud of that quarter inch.

Besides being a natural aviator, Coda also has a remarkable singing voice and recorded in Nashville in the mid-1990s with Reba McEntire's band. Actually, there's probably not much he doesn't do well—except maybe that time when he spotted what looked like one of those inflatable balls that is a favorite of kids and dogs. He shouted to a friend, "Hey, watch this!" with every intention of a full-strength kick. Building up speed on his run, he approached the ball, swung his leg full power, and *wham!* Down he went.

He's probably a little soured on bowling now. Or at least bowling balls.

One of my favorite sayings is, "If you're not living on the edge, you're taking up too much space." Despite his size, Coda Riley doesn't take up much space.

Quiet Heroes

Caution: Cape does not enable user to fly.

– Commonly attributed to a Batman costume warning label sold at Walmart, 1995

Josh Sullivan, Lifted and Gifted

Linda: On a sleepy Saturday morning at Liberty Municipal Airport, a hangar door stood open, one of the middle ones in a row of six T-hangars. Squinting through the sunlight, we scanned the shaded interior as we parked the car. "There he is." I motioned to Mike. We eagerly stepped into the hangar.

Just twelve hours earlier, we had been in that same hangar visiting with a local pilot, Randy Sullivan. "I think I'll give her a paint job for her fiftieth birthday, what ya think?" he said fondly of his Cessna 172. "Thanks to my sons saving me the college expense, I could afford this."

Randy's elder son, Jake, went to college on a baseball scholarship and his younger son, Josh, joined the military. "In fact, I have to get home soon. Josh and his wife and the grandkids are coming in for the weekend." Then he added with quiet, fatherly pride, "My son flies C-130s in the Air Force."

Seizing the opportunity, we asked if we could meet Josh. Later that evening, we negotiated the time and place: be back at the hangar tomorrow at 8:15. And now, we were about to meet one of today's heroes.

There he was, with a mountain of biceps to contrast the flatlands of Liberty, and a smile as friendly as his physique was fit.

"Hi, I'm Josh Sullivan," he said as he shook our hands. U.S. Air Force Captain, C-130 driver, Liberty, Texas, native—Joshua Sullivan. A visit with Josh is a gift in itself.

Mike: All through school Josh played baseball and football, and he powerlifted. In fact, he ranked third in the nation in powerlifting. Classmate Russel Blue told us later, "He probably didn't tell you, he was known as 'The Animal'," and teammate, Bryan McCartney, agreed. "In football, when Josh hit you, you knew it, and you never forgot it."

Before the Air Force was ever a glint in Josh's eye, he thought he'd continue playing ball in college and wasn't sure what he would do after that—that is, until Grandma had an idea.

"She's the one who got it in my head. She suggested I consider the military." Then came a grin of gratitude for Grandma. Josh would be the first in the Sullivan family to enter military service.

After graduating from Liberty High School, Josh was appointed to the U.S. Air Force Academy and immediately fit right in because, as he explained, "Dad taught us a solid work ethic, and I had a workout regimen since sixth grade, which I still do today."

The Academy years went by fast. He served in leadership positions and completed the glider and jump programs. He enjoyed flying gliders for the challenge of energy management that teaches a pilot basic aircraft control. Because there's no motor, another plane tows the glider aloft. Once it is released from the tow rope, the glider pilot takes advantage of thermal energy to ride the waves and keep the ship soaring. Josh learned there was no chance to go around if he thought he might botch the landing, so he had to get his landing right the first time.

Josh then earned an airplane private pilot certificate his senior year in a Diamond DA-20—a 125-horsepower, two-seat airplane with a stick control—and graduated with a Bachelor of Science degree.

Next came Air Force flight training at Whiting Naval Air Station, in Milton, Florida, in a T-34C Turbo Mentor. This was quite a move up from the Diamond he was flying at the academy, and Josh felt overwhelmed the first time he saw all those buttons and gauges. But the instructors taught him to compartmentalize the systems and absorb basic knowledge of the airplane in about eight weeks of ground school.

Once he was familiar with the T-34, he started training in aerobatic, instrument, and formation flight, all by the "fire hose system." We call it that because the student nearly drowns in information, guzzling down as much as possible in two years.

Aerobatics was one of his favorite phases of training, and we wanted his take on the experience. He loved the fine precision required to perfect the maneuvers, but there was also that threat of the penalty. "The instructor sat behind the student so he could smack you on the head if you messed up," he chuckled.

Mastering the skills needed to fly in tight formation with other aircraft was also a favorite. He related it to looking in the mirror. "You look over there at the other guy and see him sitting there in his cockpit, flying his airplane, and the whole sight is just so cool. Then it hits you, 'Hey, that's what I look like.' I love it. It's kind of surreal."

Once they finish that flight training, Air Force pilots choose the airplane they want to fly for their career and enter a pipeline for advanced training. Josh chose the C-130 and articulated his important reasons.

"Like all the other guys, I love the fighter jets. I flew a Strike Eagle once while in London, and I'm the right size and shape to pull the Gs. But I love the teamwork involved in a crew plane. So, while I love the speed and thrill of flying a fighter, being part of a team is better suited to me."

What he meant by "better suited" was that he knew his type-A personality could lead him down a path he didn't welcome if he chose a life that individualized him, as he believed flying fighters would. Putting his faith and family first, flying a crew plane would keep him mentally in the spirit of teamwork and cooperation.

Training in Corpus Christi in the T-44A Pegasus, the Air Force version of a King Air 90, introduced Josh to flying a twin-engine airplane. For the next eight months, he refined his skills and earned his wings as a commercial, instrument-rated pilot.

But before he could step into a front seat in the C-130, he would have to make it through four tough "weed-out" flights—designed to help officers select only the very best pilots who could handle the most difficult situations under pressure. Josh passed them all. This allowed him to move on to Little Rock, Arkansas, for a six-month initial training in the

C-130. Josh called it the four-by-four of the Air Force. The oldest models were built in 1962, a real testament to the maintenance crews.

After joining the 61st Airlift Squadron, the Green Hornets, Josh continued to hone his skills. With his crew, he practiced airdropping troops, heavy equipment, and supplies out the back of the C-130 about 300 feet off the ground over the hills of southwest Arkansas. Reading navigation charts while flying low level at night was a challenge and good practice for the combat zone, which was good since his next stop was Iraq.

He can't talk much about his time there but serving for four months on Operation Iraqi Freedom earned Josh a few months of stateside rotation. When he returned to the Middle East, he had been promoted to Aircraft Commander. His unit's main job was transporting troops, civilians, and supplies—intratheater airlift—from their main station to smaller areas within Iraq. They kept their skills sharp by practicing formation flying—but not on nice, clear days. They practiced in reduced visibility weather where pilots cannot see each other, even in close formation.

"We have to be able to drop supplies in weather without seeing the ground," he explained. "And we learn how to land that big plane in small places. All we need is a two-thousand-foot strip, and it doesn't even have to be paved. Doing this teaches us about the performance limitations of the airplane."

Our time with Josh flew by unnoticed. Suddenly, he stopped talking and raised his hand. "I want to say this: while we get shot at as we're flying low level, in and out, it's nothing like those guys in the Army and Marines. They're the ones down there with bullets whizzing by their heads every day."

He pointed as though to the cabin behind his pilot seat. "We carry these guys in the back; they are the door kickers. We appreciate everything they do. There's no glory here. Those guys are heroes. And I want that to be said."

Linda: Shifting to a lighter topic, we couldn't help but wonder what he would say was his favorite flying experience thus far. It turned out that his most memorable time in an airplane was one of the hardest things to nail down. But with all the hair-raising and exciting times he's had, the most enjoyable was probably not what you'd guess.

"I was returning from my first cross-country flight in my first phase of Air Force pilot training. I was in the front seat of a T-34C with my instructor in the back. The learning curve on this flight turned out to be pretty steep, as they are on most training flights, and things were hectic. We were en route from Houston back to Florida.

"The sun was setting, with every color one could imagine in the sky. I've seen nothing more beautiful. It may have only been sixty seconds, but it seemed like eternity. We put the training on hold for a minute and took in God's amazing view. I know how special it was because my instructor pilot, who had well over five thousand hours seeing the sky, was speechless as well."

Given that he was wearing a white t-shirt imprinted with "Lift Ministries," it was no surprise that a spectacular sunset with all the colors and glory of God's creation was his most memorable flight.

Stateside, he has worked with recovery groups, supporting, praying for, encouraging, and ministering to people with any addiction. He's played guitar for youth groups and hosted Junior Bible Quiz. "I've been involved with ministry since I was in high school. God is my life," he explained.

For Josh, flying for a living is a blessing. "While it takes a tremendous amount of work and preparation for each flight, my office is a cockpit, as opposed to a cubicle. I'm not knocking office work by any means,"—because when he's not scheduled by the squadron to fly, he's doing his fair share of office work, otherwise known in the Air Force as "additional duties"—"but it's really cool when your office has things like an airspeed indicator."

Mike: Yes, that's really cool. Ten years after serving in Operation Iraqi Freedom, Josh was promoted to Lt. Colonel, serving in the Air Force Special Operations Command. As an evaluator pilot, he instructs and provides annual evaluations to other pilots flying the C-130.

But active military duty can be rough on a family. When he leaves for another tour, his wife is at home managing five children, finances, and everything by herself. Truth is, his family sacrifices too. For Josh, his service is for more than himself or his family; it's for his country, for the entire world.

When it comes to flying, he holds dear his early days. "As blessed as I am to be involved in military aviation, I sometimes long to go back home and fly in the general aviation world. In military aviation, there's always an agenda, as there should be. We are spending taxpayer dollars to train and fight for our country. There are strict requirements we have to log to stay current on our training.

"While these are necessary, they make the times when I can get home, climb into my dad's Cessna 172, and fly around the patch an absolute joy. There's nothing like flying and just enjoying the scenery. I mean, I can't just go to work, climb into my squadron's airplane, and teach my kids the joys of flying. I can't take my family up on Christmas Eve to look at the Christmas lights from a different perspective.

"I'm sure you get the picture. I love what I do for a living, but I guess it's kind of like being a professional ballplayer. You might have an outstanding job, but it's just a little more enjoyable when you're playing ball with your kids in the backyard as opposed to making a living."

It's not just his football sacking skills or his expert control of a C-130 that make Josh Sullivan unforgettable. It's all he stands for—his faith, love for his family, duty to his country—and his kindness and humility toward a couple of local citizen pilots who were eager to hear his story and share it with you. This, friends, is the caliber of those protecting our freedoms.

Steve Fingerhut, Fighting the Good Fight

Mike: By the time he was ten years old, Steve Fingerhut knew he loved flying. He wanted to fly helicopters and held on to that dream through college and later through the police academy. Once he was on the force, the Houston police officer took advantage of the rookie night shift to take helicopter training during the day.

To enhance his flight lessons, he built a Mini 500 helicopter at home. The building experience would help him better understand how the aircraft worked.

Eventually, Steve became a commercial helicopter and multi-engine airplane pilot. With these accomplishments, the Houston Police Department offered him a position flying a Hughes 269C helicopter, and later a promotion to the Hughes 500.

The department has had an impressive safety record for their choppers – there was a broken collarbone back in 1970 – which says a lot for their training program, where pilots practice simulated autorotation during quarterly check rides.

Autorotation is landing a helicopter after an engine failure. HPD pilots rehearse autorotations in the simulator, all the way to the ground. They practice other emergency maneuvers, too, such as loss of a tail rotor in flight, maximum performance takeoffs, and ground maneuvers.

It's one thing to point the landing light at a spot on the ground and fly around it, keeping the same airspeed, altitude, and distance from the target. But when you take the wind into account, that maneuver takes concentration, and at least the pilot is facing the mark. Imagine trying to do that with your taillight: pick a point on the ground and fly a perfect circle around it using the helicopter's tail as your guide. Houston Police helicopter pilots have developed these advanced skills.

There was plenty of excitement during his nine years in HPD choppers, chasing criminals and helping capture them. When the department acquired "forward-looking infrared radar" (FLIR), Steve could see heat signatures in the dark—anything that radiated a heat differential—like people, cars, or guns. Late one night, fellow officers were walking through a field in a line, trying to find a suspect.

"They didn't know he was behind them, but I could see his heat signature. I radioed to them to stop. I noticed one person didn't stop immediately, and I identified him as the suspect. I told the officers on the ground the suspect was behind them."

Steve had spent plenty of time as one of those guys on the ground and knew the threats firsthand. Before his service in the helicopter division, he worked Houston's Third Ward night shift. Later, he oversaw the dive team for the Crime Scene Unit. And he had recovered stolen vehicles and located the thieves, whittling down the voluminous auto theft cases.

Within the Criminal Intelligence Department, he used his expertise to analyze data to capture more criminals. His equestrian skills served him well on Mounted Patrol, training fellow officers in defense tactics at the academy, and protecting dignitaries.

Steve had built a reputation, and the day after 9/11, a professional pilot training company sought his valuable experience, hiring him to set up and manage twenty-four-hour security. His success there led to several other security jobs, but even all of that is not the sum of his contributions.

Linda: In his spare time, Steve has flown for the U.S. Coast Guard Auxiliary assisting in Coast Guard search and rescue missions. He's taken mechanics and parts to downed airplanes and flown blood for patients. The latter type of flying has given him the greatest sense of contribution to his country.

"When I fly blood from Ellington Field to an interim destination, where it's carried on to Afghanistan, I know in those moments I am carrying someone's life. I don't get to meet donors or recipients—I'm just one link in the chain of help for our troops—but I *am* one link getting needed blood to people fighting terrorism. That feels good."

Steve is outspoken about the benefits of general aviation. While flying helos for work, he bought a Grumman Yankee, a small single-engine airplane, to fly for fun. He kept it at Dunham Field in Crosby and commuted to the police department hangar at Hobby Airport each day.

One day while flying back with his wife from a family visit in Louisiana, they were making good time, better than usual. There must have been a low-pressure cell moving the air from east to west. It spoiled him fast. Steve said to his wife, "I want to buy that tailwind!" That's when he moved up to a Bonanza, a jump from a Yankee in terms of power and complexity.

His Bonanza got better gas mileage than his truck, and he cut his travel time down to a fraction. Then he made another leap, this time to a fine twin-engine airplane, a Baron.

But his defense of general aviation isn't purely personal. Learning to fly makes one more valuable to the United States. That's his proverbial 30,000-foot view. Descending into details, he explains that pilots are better-educated citizens "because we've had to learn about meteorology, aerodynamics, emergency procedures, and much more. As a result, we have more to offer, such as volunteer flying to help others."

He asks where we'd be without general aviation, where we would get our military and commercial pilots. "Civilian pilot training is an integral part of general aviation. We in general aviation take the load off the airline system. General aviation creates lots of jobs and contributes billions of dollars to the economy. Post-9/11, it's not real easy to fly commercial. With the time and hassle, you have to wonder if you really want to go through all that."

To drive home the point, Steve mentioned an airline pilot friend with whom he flew to a funeral in Nebraska. "We could have taken an airliner at no cost, but time and convenience made it a poor choice for that trip, so we went in my Bonanza. We got there faster, didn't have to endure the TSA, and landed at an airport much closer to our destination."

Among the pilots who have inspired him was legendary Houston aviatrix Maybelle Fletcher. Steve humbly related the memorable personal experience taking her up in a helicopter.

It was only the second time she had ridden in a chopper but remained the longest helicopter ride she ever took. There are bragging rights in that because of who she was.

Maybelle learned to fly in 1941. Women were discouraged from flying then, yet she logged over 30,000 hours in 175 different aircraft. With a passion for teaching, she built a reputation through her three flight schools and as an FAA-designated pilot examiner. She was an aviation icon whose influence reached well beyond the Houston airspace.

"Mrs. Fletcher," as Steve called her, loved helicopters. When he took her up, they landed atop the municipal court building and the old Gulf building. Then they flew over to Dunham Field and hovered at 800 feet. Steve even showed her an autorotation.

"I thought so much of Mrs. Fletcher. She was a proper lady. She wore a dress, earrings, and heels, but she had an adventurous spirit like the heroines of her day. She was such an incredible lady."

Her combination of grace and accomplishment left an impression on Steve. But then, he notices the good in others. Perhaps he has a certain sensitivity to that because he has invested himself in humanity. He couldn't have known when he was ten where or how his desire to fly would unfold, or that it would change his life by enabling him to serve society. But now, we can see. That calling to the *thwopping* whir of rotorcraft propelled him to fight the good fight.

Charlie Sisk on Business, Aviation, and Life

Thirteen-year-old Charlie Sisk sat in the back seat of the old, white Cessna 172. He leaned forward to look around the shoulders of the pilot and front seat passenger. There were so many dials on the dashboard. Pistons whirred as the plane sped down the runway, pushing him back into his seat. The vibration from the tires rolling down the pavement suddenly was gone. Countryside and buildings scooted smoothly beneath them. A train approached a crossing and the cars stopped there looked so small. It was a short flight, maybe thirty minutes, but it changed his life.

"I got to have me one of these." That phrase would stick in his mind for nearly forty years. Then on July 4, 2006, the owner of Sisk Rifles bought his first airplane, a 1957 Cessna 182. The next thing he would need was someone to teach him to fly.

Charlie found an instructor and began flying lessons at the Cleveland airport in North Liberty County. After his first solo flight, he finished training and took his private pilot check ride at an airport near Austin.

Here was a newfound freedom that reduced travel time, and he was eager to share his joy with Aaron Baker, owner of

Cannon Safe. Certain that his friend would see the benefit, Charlie encouraged Aaron to take to the air, which he did. But the private pilot certificate wasn't enough. Aaron said didn't want to be limited to flying on cloudless days and still have to drive if weather prevented visual flight. His airplane would be more useful to him if he could fly it any time.

Therefore, to get the most out of their skill and their airplanes, Aaron suggested they get their instrument rating. The rating added to their private pilot certificates would give both businessmen the mobility they needed. Aaron proposed paying for the course if Charlie would take it first, and then help him through it. Charlie took an accelerated course and earned his instrument rating in ten days.

This master riflemaker doesn't let any grass grow under his feet. He stays busy building what customer testimonies proclaim are the most accurate rifles available. An inextricable part of his business is building lifetime relationships with his clients. He has an uncanny understanding of human behavior. His personality set the tone for his book, *Selecting and Ordering a Custom Hunting Rifle*, an entertaining read about life.

The author and gunmaker has always relied heavily on his airplane for business, philanthropy, and an occasional pleasure trip. Thanks to Aaron's encouragement, he would no longer be limited to clear weather, provided his airplane was properly equipped. Charlie needed more instruments and an instrument-certified GPS to use on gray meteorological days. In a sweet deal, he traded one of his custom-made rifles to Aaron, who traded a gun safe to someone else for a GPS for Charlie's airplane. The new device, along with a new autopilot, meant more flying days for Charlie.

On a typically productive day, Charlie could fly to Carrizo Springs, San Antonio, and Austin, deliver rifles in each city, and be home by six o'clock in the evening. Carrizo Springs is six hours one way by car, but he could make that entire trip in his Cessna 182 in less than four hours, leaving enough time to engage with clients unrushed.

"These days, it seems the notion of customer service is all but gone. Yet it has never been more important. If I didn't have an airplane, I couldn't offer as much time and attention to customers. Until you have one and use it in your business, you really don't know how valuable it is. I can't put a dollar figure on the kind of personal service my airplane allows me to provide."

Charlie knows that what's good for business is good for life, and vice versa. The same drive he has for superior customer service shows up in his philanthropic endeavors as well.

After witnessing his sister suffer from Hodgkin's disease, Charlie was uncertain whether he could handle close personal interaction with people fighting for their lives. In spite of his hesitation, Charlie joined Angel Flight, and his experiences have been uplifting. The benefits have far outweighed his previous fears.

Angel Flight coordinates volunteer pilots with patients who need transportation to medical treatment. Many cannot afford commercial travel, nor risk the exposure to germs inherent in public transportation such as airlines. For people who live far from the most prominent medical facilities, an organization such as Angel Flight may be their only hope.

That's why being part of an Angel Flight team has deep meaning to him. "When people take debilitating treatments, it takes some stress off knowing they have transportation to the doctor. As they say, getting there is half the cure."

Another reason Charlie likes flying Angel Flights is that it lets him control his giving. "I know one hundred percent is going directly to the people who need it."

Charlie also believes that getting his passengers involved in the flight may be immeasurably helpful. So whether or not he can prove the value, he takes the time to show them how to navigate using aeronautical charts and airport diagrams, as well as how to control the air vents to keep them from becoming sick during the flight.

"I think it's really helped keep the boredom down. How boring would it be to sit in a small plane for a couple of hours with nothing to do, not feeling well, and not knowing what's going on?"

He's even given them co-pilot duties, such as writing down the frequencies the controllers give. But sometimes the flight itself provides enough entertainment.

"On one flight, we had pretty rough weather all the way. I think my passenger actually found it exciting, but I was concerned. While heading to Mineral Wells, the wind was really picking up. There's no control tower there, but the people on the ground said over the radio frequency that the wind was favoring landing on the taxiway."

The two runway options were both beyond the crosswind landing limits of Charlie's airplane. "About a mile out, I banked into the wind as hard as I could, with full opposite rudder, descending to the taxiway. At about three hundred feet above the ground, the wind suddenly stopped. In front of the crowd that had gathered to see if this pilot could land in that wind, it was probably my best landing ever." That exciting flight enabled one young man to receive needed chemo treatment.

For those who don't fly or own an airplane, Charlie offers this suggestion: "You don't have to fly to help. Ground volunteers are needed too. People with clerical or administrative skills, ground transportation, a cheerful attitude, and a caring smile are needed. You don't need flying skills for that."

Charlie's got a heart for people. He's taken his assets and put them to use to help others. That one short flight he took as a young teenager not only changed his life but has touched many others since.

A Life Saved, Thanks to an Airport

Mike: Airports are important for interstate commerce and economic growth, but often an airport's value is immeasurable. Just ask the King family.

The week before Easter, Gayden King, a fifty-five-year-old man with Down syndrome, visited three of his sisters in Liberty, Texas. While their parents stayed home in Louisiana, Brenda, LaDell, and Garnet were happy to have their brother here and to offer their parents a respite. The sisters expected to see Gayden excitedly take part in coloring Easter eggs and anticipating the upcoming holiday. But he seemed too tired to enjoy the activities.

Soon, tired turned into lethargic and Gayden's behavior became uncharacteristic. He called his sisters by the wrong names and had no interest in the festivities. Something wasn't right, so the women drove their precious brother to the emergency room. On the way, Gayden stopped breathing.

The doctors revived him, diagnosed him with pneumonia, and gave antibiotics and advice: He should be taken back to Louisiana, to his own doctors. People with Down syndrome have many health problems, and medical professionals familiar with the patient are better suited to care for them.

"Few doctors would treat an older man from out of state with Down syndrome whose medical history they were not familiar with," Brenda explained.

Since the hour was late, Brenda and her sisters thought it best to begin their trip first thing in the morning. But Gayden's condition deteriorated, and they returned to the emergency room in the middle of the night. While they discussed what to do, their parents and two brothers drove overnight to Liberty. As his condition worsened, the doctors warned the family that Gayden's kidneys were failing. He would not make the five-hour car trip to Louisiana.

Linda: Brenda wrote us this note: "Because we are blessed in Liberty to have an airport, we could make plans to get Gayden home. We hired an air ambulance from New Orleans. A Liberty airport employee opened the gates for our family to be together as Gayden was put on the plane. It meant so much to us because we didn't know if we would ever see our brother again."

Another sister was waiting in Hammond to meet the plane and accompany Gayden to the hospital where his doctors waited. A month later, Gayden King won his battle with pneumonia and kidney failure and returned home to his parents, where he lived for another thirteen years.

Brenda represented the family's thoughts of gratitude: "Gayden was a blessing for our family, and we are thankful we could love and care for him for so long."

One of her brothers added, "I am so thankful for that small airport in Liberty because without it, we may have lost Gayden then, and what a tragedy that would have been."

The airport gave the King family more time to love on Gayden, with thirteen more Easters, thirteen more Christmases, and many more times to celebrate life together.

Police Chiefs

Linda: When federal funds became available for small communities like Daisetta, Texas, to afford more police, Les Hulsey applied for the job where his flying skills came in handy. Before becoming the Daisetta Police Chief, Les took flight lessons at Helicopter Services at Hooks Airport in Tomball. But his history in aviation goes further back.

As a U.S. Army sergeant, Les spent many hours aboard military helicopters. He was a gunner on daily resupply missions over the Cambodia-Laos border during the Vietnam War in 1972–73. On the back of his neck is a graphic scar from injuries he received when his chopper was shot down. He and four comrades spent three days running from the enemy near the river banks. They hid in the forest until U.S. forces retrieved them and returned them to their base in Thailand.

"They teach the pilots to roll the helicopter over, so we're less likely to be cut up by the blades. So we rolled over into the trees, and all got out," he said matter-of-factly.

After leaving the Army, the adrenaline rush would be hard to match, but eventually Les became a Houston firefighter where at times he would rappel from a helicopter on rescue missions. Upon retirement, he went to work for the Harris County Sheriff Department. His assignment in crime prevention included a few years running Rice University's rape defense program, one of his most personally rewarding jobs.

But even in this life of service to others, the thrill of flying kept calling. The thought of being airborne would spread his thick goatee to make room for a contagious smile. "Back when I was a gunner, I took flying for granted. After I left the Army, I really missed it."

Serving the citizens of Daisetta, as a student pilot Les flew with an instructor in a Robinson R44 helicopter to assist in the search for escaped prisoners. He also caught poachers who killed an alligator in the wetlands.

While Les Hulsey proved an aviator in law enforcement could be a dangerous thing for criminals, another local officer told a different story, showing us there's also room for humor.

Mike: When former Liberty Police Chief Mike Cummings worked for the Houston Police Department, after work he would often go to Westheimer Air Park and rent an airplane for an evening flight.

One afternoon, he invited a friend to fly with him to Brenham for dinner. The Southern Flyer Diner is a 1950s-style restaurant with a patio that faces the Brenham Municipal Airport runway. Folks come to watch planes take off and land and enjoy the relaxed atmosphere and great food. A popular spot, Brenham's airport was named the Texas Department of Transportation's Airport of the Year in 2004, contributing millions of dollars per year to the community.

It was a short flight from the Westheimer Air Park to Brenham, but on this date, it was an interesting one. The Chief takes it from here.

Chief Cummings: I started the engine and just before taxiing to the run-up area, my buddy dropped something on the floor. There's not much room in a Cessna 172, so he got out of the airplane to find whatever it was he lost. Once he found it and was back in and shut the door, I taxied onto the engine run-up area on the ramp.

After checking flight controls and instruments, everything looked fine. But as I increased the RPMs for the magneto check, suddenly we heard *Bang! Bang-Bang-Bang!* A thorough recheck of all instruments told me nothing was amiss. I decreased the throttle, and the noise went away. Figuring all was good, we took off for Brenham.

Shortly after takeoff, however, the noise returned. *Bang! Bang-Bang!* More concerned now that we were in the air, I said, "You look outside. See if anything's falling off the airplane. I'll check the instruments."

Nothing registered out of the ordinary, and my passenger didn't report any de-parting. But the noise didn't go away this time. So I did what any prudent captain would do. I prepared for an emergency landing. Being nightfall, Highway 290 looked like the best alternative to a runway.

Bang! Bang-Bang! "We're going down!" I shouted.

Descending to 1,400 feet...1,200 feet...1,000 feet above the highway, my passenger suddenly gasped, "Ah! I think it's my seatbelt!" Quickly, he opened the door to confirm and retrieve the wayward noisemaker.

Shoving the throttle in quickly, I gave it full power to return to 3,000 feet, relieved we didn't have to land on the highway.

Can't you just imagine the FAA investigator? "And just what caused this emergency landing, Mr. Cummings? What's this? A seatbelt?!"

Mike: If you fly, the moral of the story is, remember to read your checklist, which includes safety belts and shoulder harnesses. If you don't fly, you might want to note that Chief Cummings is keenly interested in seat belts being fastened, in the air and on the ground.

Peruvian Lights

Linda: In Liberty, we're fortunate to have an airport and a couple of helipads. As publicly owned assets, it's their job to serve the community, which they do, night and day.

A story from eastern Peru makes me think of the Kings, a local family who shared their experience of how Liberty Airport played a role in rescuing their brother, Gayden. Like the Kings, one Peruvian family is grateful for their runway, the airplane, the pilot, and the whole community.

Contamana is a remote town in the rain forest, one of the poorest places in Peru. Their airport is the lifeline to the outside world. It was one night in April 2013, when a new young mom struggled through childbirth. The baby was born, but there were complications threatening both mother and child. The mother's condition turned critical, but the town's hospital was not equipped to handle her situation. An emergency medical flight would have to take them immediately to Pucallpa, seventy-eight miles away.

However, Contamana's small airport had only basic facilities, and no lights, making a night takeoff from their local landing field unsafe. The runway was 2,600 feet long. By comparison, the Liberty Airport is 3,800 feet. There would be no wiggle room—they would have to lift off the ground in very little distance. The pilot of the Cessna Caravan considered his passengers' safety and determined they could not depart from such a short, unimproved runway in the jungles of Peru in total darkness.

But in that remote little town there is also a local radio station, which I imagine is run by a person like Bill Buchanan, who founded KSHN radio in Liberty; someone who cares and doesn't just stand by, shaking his head, saying, "Somebody ought to do something."

The good folks at the radio station learned of the situation and the DJ went without delay to the airwaves, asking listeners for help. I know our local station would do the same.

But how could the people of this remote town in Peru help their neighbors in need? Their response will warm your heart.

Mike: Within minutes of the DJ sending out the plea, taxi drivers and people from across the listening area drove their cars, motorbikes, and auto-rickshaws to the airfield. Three hundred vehicles lined up along both sides and drivers shone their headlights to light up the runway.

Thanks to the unselfishness of all those people who dropped everything they were doing to rush to the airport and light the way to hope and healing, the airplane could take off with mama and baby on board. Bystanders cheered, and people knew they had done what was right at the time it was needed, their help having saved two lives.

Small Airports Give Life

Linda: Often I wonder what led a person to become a pilot. In Jason Talley's case, the Red Barn restaurant had something to do with it—the peppermint ice cream, too; both are inviting to a young boy. Add the intrigue of activity at a grass airfield and the comfort of family Sunday afternoons, and the result just may turn out to be the proper recipe for a future pilot.

For as long as he can remember, Jason wanted to fly. A smart kid, his grades won him scholarships and within a couple of years of high school graduation, he'd built and sold his first technology company. Four years and three companies later, mathematics degree in hand, he took a hiatus and learned to fly.

What would be next for Jason after earning a pilot certificate? Law school seemed a fitting choice. If he ever needed a fallback occupation, he could always practice law.

After passing the state bar in his home state of Missouri, he passed the Kansas and California bars. Delightful West Coast weather convinced Jason to move his family to California where he continued as a serial entrepreneur and added to his pilot certificate and ratings. He earned the highest level pilot and instructor certificates. Then he bought a jet—a Citation Mustang.

When I asked what he'd want most for people to know about aviation, he didn't hesitate. "That a lot of general aviation pilots are passionate, not only about flying but doing things for others also."

Jason puts his passion to work and makes a great example. Among the charitable organizations he helps, with Veterans Airlift Command, he can get veterans to airports that airlines don't serve—airports closer to where they live. They provide free flights for medical and other compassionate purposes to combat-wounded and their families.

"Our military veterans have given us the best years of their lives, and general aviation provides a mechanism where we can say 'Thank you.'"

Likewise, with Angel Flight, Jason takes people of all ages to where they need to be for medical treatment. These special passengers don't necessarily live far from a major airport, but for many, riding on an airliner poses a threat to their health. Private flying is a critical solution.

Donating time, fuel, money, and an aircraft to fly someone who needs help is near to Jason's heart. It has also given him an immense appreciation for small airports, and he points out, "This outreach ceases to be possible when community airports don't receive public support."

As a member of Angel Flight's board of directors, Jason especially appreciates the annual awards dinners. "It's so neat to see our volunteer pilots at these dinners where, at each table, someone who has benefited from an Angel Flight is also seated. When they share their story with the group, you know you gave something of immeasurable value to someone, to their family. Maybe it was a little more time; maybe it was another chance."

Giving someone something they may not have otherwise had—a chance for survival, or more time with their family—is as good for the volunteering pilots as it is for the patients and their loved ones.

As a businessman, Jason couldn't do what he does with any efficiency if he had to rely on airlines. By flying himself, he gets to spend more time with his wife and their young sons.

"That's important, too," urges the boy who loved Sunday afternoon family dinners at the Red Barn restaurant beside the grass strip where small planes took off and landed—and the peppermint ice cream was the best in the world.

Uncaged

Birds born in a cage think flying is an illness.

—Alejandro Jodorowsky

If it be so, then we, Linda and I, are incurable.

—Mike Ely

Riding the Thermals

Mike: Our glider leaned to the side, the long wing's tip touching the ground, as normal for a glider at rest. I was in the front seat. My instructor, Jason Stephens, sat behind me, ready for our flight. The tow plane moved gently forward, tightening the rope that connected us. When taut, I wagged my rudder to signal to the tow pilot that I was ready. He wagged his rudder in response and pushed his throttle forward. His prop kicked up a cloud of dust, but it was light enough to see through as we rolled down the runway.

The small wingtip wheel scraped the ground. As we gained speed, the flight controls became effective, allowing me to lift the wing and balance on the main wheel below the fuselage. With drag reduced, we accelerated quickly and the sailplane yearned to be airborne.

I couldn't let the glider fly yet because doing so would pull the tow plane's tail up, causing it to flip. Instead, I kept the glider inches above the ground until the tow plane reached flying speed and took us skyward. Because of the rope's tension, I felt every jolt and bounce magnified. The acceleration and incline pushed me back into the seat.

After reaching our agreed-upon altitude, I pulled the knob to release us from the umbilical. The rope furled away. I raised the nose and banked to the right. The tow plane made a diving left turn to return to the glider port.

Pilots often seek new challenges with different types of flying to hone their skills and keep fresh perspectives. Soaring in gliders is one way of learning energy management and developing a keener sense of meteorology.

Gliders are always descending. When the air is rising faster than the glider's descent through it, the glider actually gains altitude. We call that *lift*. After the tow release, it's possible for a glider to stay aloft for hours. We take advantage of lift from thermals, wind over ridges, and mountain waves. The glider pilot becomes skilled at identifying lift, such as thermal activity.

One indication of thermal activity is the dust devil. During late spring through fall in the southwestern United States, these columns of dust can extend skyward several hundred feet, looking like tornadoes. These dust devils are signposts for gliders, saying, "Here is lift! Come and get it!"

Disney's *The Boy Who Flew with Condors* opens with a kid scaling a rocky ledge to gain a better vantage point of condors in flight. Their grand wings catch updrafts and they soar in lazy circles. A glider landing in a nearby field diverts his attention. He climbs down to meet the pilot. As the ground crew loads the glider onto a trailer, the pilot invites the boy to their airport to learn about soaring.

The story follows his journey as he learns to fly. He pursues achievement badges and awards such as the Diamond badge for long-distance, cross-country flight. When a rainstorm threatens his flight, the condors help him find lift.

I was enthralled by anything that involved flying, but Disney's film helped plant that seed at an early age.

We made a shallow bank to keep our sailplane in the middle of a thermal. We were on the lookout for other gliders. The lift one discovers may be all there is for miles around and, if it is strong, everybody wants some. While few gliders were riding the airwaves over Maricopa, Arizona, that did not mean we wouldn't have company.

While soaring in the rising air, a red-tailed hawk appeared beside us. It hovered a few feet from the canopy. The raptor not only wanted to share our lift but liked the shady spot it found under our much longer wing. This magnificent hawk, with broad, round wings and a short, wide tail, flew alongside, not ten feet away.

When flying jets, I avoid birds, not fly in formation with them! I banked in for a turn to keep circling in the updraft, but the hawk banked with us, its wings changing shape. The feathers around its trailing claws fluttered in the air as the awesome bird stayed almost precisely the same distance from us at all times.

After a few minutes, Jason suggested we carefully turn away from the thermal, warning, "It would be bad karma to hit a hawk." Wishing to avoid a collision, I saved the memory, leaving the thermal to this majestic bird. For a moment, it followed, then broke in the opposite direction, back to the lift to resume its post over the wide, open desert.

No words were uttered as we returned to the glider port. We marveled at having soared in formation with this mighty bird of prey, as though it had welcomed us as comrades.

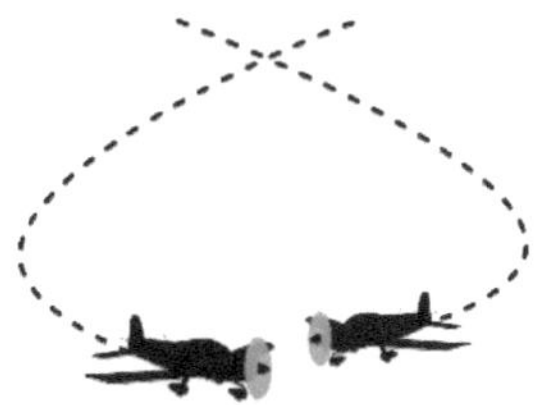

Gypsy Week

Linda: The week from Christmas to New Year's offered time to get away, a calling to my inner gypsy. With weather in some parts of the country behaving wretchedly, we pledged to go where the sun was shining. We had no particular plans other than feeding our craving for flight, so on toward nice weather we flew—*westward ho!*

The afternoon spread across the West Texas plains. The last hour of our flight extended past sunset, with residual light shining upon Guadalupe Peak for fifty miles. Las Cruces, New Mexico, seemed like a good place to stop for the night.

We called fellow air racer Seth Baker, who lived there. This is one of the things about the community of aviators—we know people all over the country, making it easy to connect with someone in almost any city. Seth is a good friend with a great sense of humor. His airplane race number in the Sport Air Racing League was B4U.

He offered a warm welcome, shared a couple of meals, and gave us a pleasant sendoff the next morning.

Away from Las Cruces, along the playa just west of Lordsburg, some areas were still soggy from recent rains. The

Peloncillo Mountains, those layered rock formations established over millennia from ash and basalt from eruptions, erosion, and eruptions again, stood proudly along the Arizona-New Mexico line. There, in Skeleton Canyon, Geronimo surrendered to the United States Cavalry.

While it was rainy and cloudy back in Liberty, we were soaking in the sunshine. My personal historian and geographer offered thoughtful narratives about the areas below as we took turns flying.

Mike: Arid deserts surround the Chiricahua Mountains. I've climbed this range and find the nickname, "Sky Islands" appropriate. They rise from the brown desert floor to their 9,759-foot peak. The temperature decreases and vegetation turns green. Pine trees stand up to 70 feet tall, like an oasis in a desert sea. Flying over the foothills at 8,500 feet, those pines at their highest point were still higher than we were.

Pushing into the headwind, we traveled further west with Cochise's Stronghold in the Dragoon Mountains to our left. Then crossing a ridge into the Tucson area, we skirted high mountains, turning north. Finding a hotel in Phoenix would be easy.

After a night in the Valley of the Sun, Flagstaff called. Dear friends picked us up at the airport and welcomed us with warm hearts to their "mile-and-a-quarter-high city." As we drove out to their remote property, I realized how much I missed mountain air. After joining them for worship services Sunday morning, we flew to Boulder City, Nevada, where my brother and his family live.

The mighty Colorado River rushed beneath us and steep canyon walls concealed the massive Boulder Dam until we were almost on top of it. In this area it's important to keep a constant watch, scanning the horizon for planes and helicopters full of tourists returning from the Grand Canyon. We stayed clear of parachute jumpers and mixed in easily with the rest of the traffic.

After landing and tying down the *Elyminator*, we came to the home of my brother and sister-in-law. The evening's entertainment was provided by their four highly animated, homeschooled grandchildren.

The six-year-old theatrically whispered the secret that her four-year-old sister would need our help in a family game. With a hand to one side of her face, the older child shielded the potentially insulting words. She leaned in close to us. Her blue eyes widened, and her mouth engaged her entire face to enunciate each sound with hushed intensity: "...because reading is involved!"

The next day, more educated than when we arrived, we said our adieus and headed south along the Colorado River.

Here was Lake Havasu and its island. Remnants of the old airport that had been on the island stirred up mixed feelings. Built by Robert McCulloch, the chainsaw manufacturer, it was the neatest little airport. That is, until those gambling-zone speculators got their paws on it. The island airport had been such a joy to fly in to, but they argued casinos would be a better use of the land. Nostalgia lost. But in the end, aviation won. A new airport was built north of the city, and the charlatans never did get their casinos.

And here was the link Mr. McCulloch added to reach his airport. It was the old London Bridge, which was falling down, he had shipped here from England and reassembled.

It connects the island to the city, which used to be small and quaint. Now, sunlight glimmers off houses shoved into canyons and stacked up hillsides.

Two-hundred-fifty miles beyond the lovely blue water of Havasu is Benson, Arizona, home of veterinarian-turned-cowboy poet Baxter Black, who broadcasts a weekly radio program.

Benson is familiar to us. With the airplane tied down, we took the courtesy shuttle to the hotel where we get the pilot discount. We didn't know that Seth Baker had flown there too. He admitted in a text early the next morning, he didn't hide our plane in a hangar and leave a treasure map on the ground only because he wouldn't be there to witness the ambush.

Roy Jones is the face of Benson for travelers stopping in. He runs the FBO and sets a great example. He sells fuel, gives flight lessons, and helps whenever needed. The most unique thing about this fuel stop is Roy's tradition: a fuel discount for a clean joke he can tell his children. We know this, yet we usually don't remember until we're flying the last leg there.

The conversation in the cockpit then turns to, "We need a joke!" followed by brainstorming. One joke we offered was, "What happens when a frog's car breaks down? It gets toad away." That was good enough for the fuel discount.

The next morning's flight took us over Reserve, New Mexico and on to Albuquerque for lunch, then a hop into Santa Fe in time for New Year's Eve. This is probably a good place for a New Year's party, but such things require plans. This was fine with us. Like the barnstormers of old, we wayfarers are happier to swap an RSVP for an unscripted adventure.

The first day of the New Year, we reluctantly headed back to the real world. The 57-knot tailwind across the Rockies created up and downdrafts we felt for over 160 miles.

With the wind at our back, we agreed—gypsy week should happen again.

Island Hopping

Linda: Orcas Island and Friday Harbor, part of the San Juan Islands off the coast of Washington State, were excellent choices for adventure flying right after receiving my private pilot certificate.

The largest of the San Juans, Orcas Island's 2,900 by 60-foot north-south asphalt runway crosses the east-west-shaped island for most of its width.

I thought the island's name was derived from the whales playing offshore. But "Orcas" is a shortened form of Juan Vicente de Güemes Padilla Horcasitas y Aguayo, Second Count of Revillagigedo, the viceroy of Mexico. Thank goodness someone shortened it. He's an important fellow worthy of the honor because he sent an exploration expedition under Francisco de Eliza to the Pacific Northwest in 1791.

The annual fly-in to Orcas Island is the first weekend in August. It's an invitation to camp next to your aircraft and enjoy good food, entertainment, and shopping in the village of Eastsound. Proceeds from the pancake breakfast benefit the Orcas Island Volunteer Firefighter/EMT Association. Camping and parking are free. The Orcas Island Community Band entertains the crowd, and an antique car show brings in more visitors.

Friday Harbor Island's runway is 3,400 feet long and 75 feet wide. There's a U.S. Customs port of entry and a seaplane base. The airport planners hold their meetings at Ernie's Café, named in honor of Ernest K. Gann, the famed aviator and author of many novels and movies, such as *The High and the Mighty*.

A few minutes' walk to downtown offers great choices in shops and eateries. A fifteen-minute walk in another direction takes you to the port's marina, where you can catch a ride out on the water, check out the whales, and listen to live music.

Hikers and cyclists enjoy the two-mile Clark McAlpine Trail along the west side of the airport. Boy Scout Troop 90 helped build the scenic route and later added a loop trail, which extends through airport property to Skagit Valley College.

I've visited the islands a few times, first with instructors and later with a friend who was an air traffic controller on the mainland in Bellingham.

During my island-hopping flight with Grady, one of Bellingham Aero's instructors, the aerial views of lighthouses triggered a history lesson. "You know about the Pig War, right?"

"No," I told him. That was left out of Indiana history when I went to school.

"Well, the U.S. and Great Britain disagreed over the U.S.-Canada border in the San Juan Islands, between Vancouver Island and the mainland. British and Americans were living on the island, and an American shot a pig that was eating his potatoes."

The short version is that the pig's British owner was pretty upset. The American offered $10, but the pig owner demanded $100. The Brits were going to arrest the American, and then both militaries got involved. "But no one other than the pig was killed," Grady explained.

In the longer version, I learned it was 1859 and the argument escalated, ending with fourteen American cannons opposing three British warships with seventy guns on board. British soldiers outnumbered Americans by more than four to one. Each was willing to defend, but neither would fire the first shot.

When officials of both countries learned of the war threat over a potato-stealing pig, the standoff ceased. The English settled on the north end of the island, the American camp on the south. Years later, an international arbitration commission decided the border dispute, siding with the U.S. So, in some way, perhaps I owed that poor hungry pig a thank you that I didn't have to file an international flight plan just to go island hopping off the Northwest coast.

But a pig wasn't the only animal in this story. As a private pilot without much time logged, lofty whale watching provided a new perspective where I could witness the beautiful mammals in their Salish Sea playground. As coastal views go, the San Juan Islands offered more panoramic beauty than the industrial vista near Galveston Bay, where I was introduced to flying. Majestic Mount Baker was a more refreshing landmark than the smokestacks of south Houston. While these island runways don't offer the same challenge to landing as Catalina Island, it was island hopping, and it offered some of the best social aviation atmosphere in the Pacific Northwest.

Mike: I took my first cross-country flight as a new private pilot from El Monte, California, to Catalina Island, landing at the "Airport in the Sky." Now, there was an adventure.

Catalina Island is twenty-one miles long and about eight miles across at its widest point. The island has two distinct parts, separated by an isthmus about half a mile wide. The airport is built atop a cut-off hill. Sixteen hundred feet above sea level, it drops off steeply to the ocean at either end.

From the air, the airport almost looks like an aircraft carrier. The first two-thirds of the runway slope uphill and the last third levels out. On close-in final approach, the last thousand feet on the other end are not visible. This makes the runway look incredibly short just as one is about to land.

Back then, most airplane rental operations required no specific training to fly to Catalina Island, but as per my description above, I can understand why that's changed. Taking that first trip with a person experienced with Catalina's special characteristics would have been nice. My brother Doug and our friend Tim accompanied me for a day trip.

On final approach, I fell for the illusion and thought I wouldn't make it. I applied takeoff power and climbed out again, making a go-around. I flew the traffic pattern, set up on final again, and this time a gust of wind bumped us up in the air, causing me to make another go-around. On the third attempt, the airplane settled smoothly onto the runway, and we used barely half of the available real estate with little braking needed before stopping. Third time's a charm.

Avalon, the only town, is ten miles from the airport on the southeastern side of the island. The switchback road descends into Avalon where most of Catalina's citizens live. A seat on the shuttle van offered a ride as unique as the island's runway. Our driver dodged wild buffalo set loose by a movie company after filming on the island in the 1920s.

I have since made over fifty trips to Catalina Island, mostly as a flight instructor showing others how to land there. But on this trip, I had to endure the rest of the day as Tim ribbed me with comments to total strangers that "this is the guy who buzzed the airport three times."

The Honeymoon

Mike: An autumn honeymoon in Maine was ours, amid varied coastal terrain around Blue Hill, Bar Harbor, and Acadia National Park. We took in scenic views from the ground and air. Linda had her first chance to fly a seaplane from a little lake near Bangor, and I rode along snapping pictures of vivid fall colors and a big smile with each splashdown.

Linda: There we were, driving around Maine when we spotted a seaplane overhead. Now, a couple of newlywed pilots can't just let that go without investigating. Excited and determined to find the seaplane base, we drove until we discovered it: a lake with all kinds of planes on floats. There were a couple of Cessna 180s and 185s, a 182 and a 172, a Citabria, and two Piper Super Cubs. Could we fly one?

We called the phone number listed on a little shack. The owner of a Cessna 180, who also happened to be an instructor, walked out from a nearby house. He offered me the left seat, and I jumped in. Mike already had his seaplane rating and was happy to see me fly one.

Learning to fly a seaplane is a little different, mainly for taxi, takeoff, and landing as you get the feel of piloting a boat-like vehicle until airborne. Be careful of the waves and pull the yoke back to keep the prop out of the water, lest it dip in and flip the airplane over. Beginning the takeoff run, I was taught to feel for the "step" as you would in a boat, increasing the throttle accordingly. Lifting off the water, we climbed into the cool fall air.

Red, orange, green, and golden hues of maple leaves laughed from the tickling of the wind. A tapestry of scattered lakes, ponds, and quaint villages with church steeples and country roads spread beneath us. We flew to a small pond where I could practice takeoffs and landings; I logged four.

You sit up a little higher in a plane on floats, so the cockpit view when descending requires gauging how high you'll be when the floats touch the water. It's a different sight picture because depth perception descending to water is different than landing on a runway. And as pilots know, the pitch attitude on touchdown is flatter in a seaplane. I was getting the hang of it, and Mike and the instructor both said I did well.

Mike: Thrilled with her first seaplane experience, the following day we took a ride in the back seat of a glider—another first for my new bride. She says it was on this ride she learned something about herself. While she appreciates that gliders are an excellent way to improve flying skill through managing energy of a non-motorized aircraft, trading speed for altitude and altitude for speed, I have some convincing to do to get her back in one.

After entering four splashdowns in her logbook, the ink was barely dry when Linda climbed into the glider. Wedged into the back seat of this supposedly three-person glider, we felt like we were crammed into a one-person bathtub.

Gliders are launched by another airplane towing them to a preplanned altitude. Or, less commonly, self-launched using a small engine that retracts upon reaching the desired altitude. Here, we would be towed aloft for a bird's-eye view of Acadia National Park.

Once the ground crew closed and latched the Plexiglas canopy, our pilot wiggled the rudder, signaling we were ready. The tow plane pilot echoed the sign and powered up for takeoff.

When accelerating down the runway, the glider lifts off the ground first. The glider pilot keeps it flying close to the ground until the heavier tow plane breaks from gravity's grip. The glider stays about two hundred feet behind the tow plane until released. The flight is almost silent except for the slight sound of air rushing by and any chatter between us. But here's Linda's impression of her first glider flight.

Linda: Air? After the canopy was closed and latched, I snapped a few quick photos and thought, *Yikes! It's tight back here!*

Our pilot, Jeff, briefed us as the tow plane took the runway. Soon we were airborne, with Mike and I squished in the back seat. With no grounding elements of engine vibration and noise, and no airflow, it felt as though we were floating, suspended in the air, a dizzying feeling. A few minutes into the flight, I sputtered, "I need air." Jeff pointed a small vent toward me, but it wasn't enough. I needed to get on the ground quickly or I'd lose my cookies all over the back of Jeff's head.

He pulled the rope release, and we turned away from the tow plane and back toward the airport. Moving made me feel better, and I am convinced now that I was made to do aerobatics, not to hang in the air. Captain Jeff made the rest of our ride suited to my liking, catching thermals to do wingovers, not-so-lazy-eights, and semi-aerobatic maneuvers, and suddenly I wasn't sick anymore!

Mike: While Linda's introduction to "silent flight" wasn't what she expected, it is a sport many enjoy, including races and other competition.

Linda: I figured since Mike enjoys soaring, I could be a tow pilot. That is, until I learned tow pilots need a minimum of three glider flights per year to stay current. Maybe I'll try it again sometime, because learning soaring skills will make me a better pilot—but next time, I'd better make sure I have plenty of air.

A Cub and a Moth

Linda: The Texas hill country beckoned with its winding rivers, lakes with sandbars, and abundance of ranches for grass landing strips. This was the perfect place for a Piper Super Cub, and November brought ideal weather for getting that tailwheel endorsement in my logbook. I took my instruction from Ken Wittekiend of ProMark Aviation Services in Burnet.

Mike: These days, most new pilots train in an airplane with a nosewheel, such as a Cessna 172. An airplane with a free-castering tailwheel can make for some exciting landings if one hasn't learned to handle a taildragger, hence the requirement for special training. If you don't use the rudders to keep the tailwheel airplane straight when taxiing, taking off, or landing, the tail can swing around in front of you. It's like losing control of a bicycle with hand brakes, or when a truck jackknifes.

There was a time when all airplanes were taildraggers, like the DC-3s, Stearmans, and Tiger Moths. But new designs, dubbed "tricycle gear," moved the center of gravity forward, reducing the threat of ground loops.

Linda: There wasn't much wind to practice crosswind landing in, so Ken had me fast-taxi up on one wheel to simulate wind coming at me from one side. Like a side-wheelie. That part was a breeze, so he let me move on to do some fun flying.

I skimmed the treetops along the banks of the Llano River, showing off my first experience in a Super Cub to a few herds of cattle, deer, and wild pigs. We flew low over the Colorado River, and when campers waved their hats, I rocked my wings in reply.

Ken has several friends who let him use their strips for training. Fortunately, one of our ranch landings was just in time, as the two large glasses of water from lunch were taking effect. Ranch owners Len and Beth, a ranch hand, and a dog greeted us as we taxied up. There is no graceful way to enter or exit a Cub, but one can do it quickly when necessary. As long as I missed the fresh patties, Ken found my predicament amusing.

After six hours and twenty landings on grass strips, sandbars, cow pastures, and ranches, plus ripped jeans from an ungraceful dismount, I earned my hoped-for endorsement with high praise from an outstanding instructor. Now if only I could find a Tiger Moth to fly. The Tiger Moth is the taildragger I've wanted to fly since I first read about it.

While somewhere in Europe, our world-traveling pilot friend, Jed Keck, sent me a copy of Sheila Scott's autobiography, *I Must Fly*. I found I had many things in common with the late British aviatrix, like her competitive spirit, love of all things aviation, and appreciation for friendly people.

Sheila broke over one hundred aviation records from 1965 to 1971, including three around-the-world flights in a Piper Comanche. Building up to that skill and stamina, she learned to fly in a de Havilland Gipsy Moth, a fabric-covered biplane used as a military trainer in the 1930s. She also flew a similar model, the Tiger Moth.

Being the cool chick pilot she was, she nicknamed her first airplane *Myth* because it means female moth. Over the years, Sheila dubbed her planes *Myth, Myth Too, Sun Myth Pip,* and *Mythre*. The word "Myth" was always written somewhere on any plane she flew, even if only in lipstick, and even if it wasn't a Moth. She had some close calls and sometimes was surprised her airplane was still flying. She attributed her good fortune to the name *Myth*.

I love her competitive spirit. Funny thing about the Moth, though, is the year before I was gifted the book about Sheila, another good friend, Katie Jarrett, gave me the autobiography of Bette Bach Fineman, *Patterns*. Bette is a long-time friend of Katie and her family. Katie had her sign the book to me at the annual Antique Aircraft Association Fly-In in Blakesburg, Iowa. Bette's name "Bach" comes from her longtime marriage to writer Richard Bach. She's no stranger to aviation.

In *Patterns,* Bette wrote about flying a Gipsy Moth. She loved that airplane, and the way she wrote made me wish I had one, or at least the chance to fly one. That desire grew after reading Sheila Scott's book.

Katie's stepmom, Sharon, told me the previous year that if I'd come to Blakesburg, I might have a good chance of seeing a Gipsy Moth or Tiger Moth. Maybe I'd even get a ride. We reserved that date on our calendar right away.

The months rolled by and soon it was September again, time for the Antique Aircraft Fly-In. I had "Myth" on my mind.

About a week before the fly-in, the timing of another commitment changed, disrupting our plans. Disappointed, I headed to work on the very Friday morning we should have been flying to Blakesburg. Locals will appreciate that I first stopped for gas at John Hebert's gas station in front of Thrif-Tee Foods.

On the middle pump, a huge orange-ish butterfly with interesting markings caught my eye. It didn't seem to be bothered by my pumping gas and didn't move when I took its picture, which I texted to Mike with the suggestion that if he needed gas, he should go to the middle pump and check out the butterfly with a ten-inch wingspan.

"I don't know how to tell you this," he messaged back, "but that's not a butterfly."

"It's not?" It sure looked like a butterfly.

"No." He paused. "That's a Tiger Moth."

Fall Foliage Flying Tour

Mike: After planning for over a year, we took off in our Cheetah for a New England leaf-peeping tour. The rolling terrain dressed in beautiful fall splendor of ash, birch, and maple draws many foliage fans every year. Sojourning with the birds grants a great view of the countryside from Houston to Boston.

Leaving the flatness of Southeast Texas, we marveled at God's handiwork. The Smokey, Pocono, Catskill, Berkshire, and Adirondack mountains each offered their beauty. Winging our way northeast from a fuel stop in Chattanooga, the landscape changed from green and brown to shouts of yellow, orange, and red, becoming more brilliant as we crossed over West Virginia into Maryland.

Cumberland, Maryland, was our lunch stop. Gusty winds made the landing sporty. An adorable little town with a population of about twenty thousand, their historic shopping, and restaurant district downtown is impressive with its brick streets, flowerpot-lined sidewalks, and interesting architecture.

Linda: Following a scrumptious meal, we were off to Bedford, our Boston-area destination airport. In the air, New York Center controllers rattled a steady stream of traffic instructions to pilots. They gave advisories about airline arrivals crossing our path flying into New York's busy airports. A typical transmission sounded like, "Grumman Niner Fife Eight, traffic, eleven o'clock, three miles, eastbound at fife thousand feet, a 747."

A little further north, we could see West Point Military Academy along the Hudson River. I said something to Mike about trying a water landing—Sully style. He'd already had his moment of imposter-glory when he recreated that famous scene in a simulator. I remember the grin as he told me he'd landed "within a block of Sully's landing"—in the sim.

Mike: Assisted by a speedy tailwind, we sailed through New York and Boston's airspace, flew over Walden Pond—made famous by Henry David Thoreau—and entered the traffic pattern at Bedford, Massachusetts. We had reservations in nearby Concord at the historic Colonial Inn, which proudly faces Monument Park, the centerpiece of Concord's downtown.

There stands a monument to the area's patriots who hoped for peace but had to fight when the British Redcoats attempted to take over the town on April 19, 1775. It was in that spot people gathered and waited as the king's soldiers marched from Boston to Lexington, then headed to Concord. Many of the original taverns, meeting houses, and residences are still standing.

In Lexington, seven miles east of Concord, the British had opened fire, killing eight and injuring many more. The people of Lexington didn't shoot back. Among the wounded was Prince Estabrook, a black slave who served in the local militia.

He was the first black soldier to fight in the American Revolution. A memorial honors him "and thousands of other courageous black patriots long denied the recognition they deserve."[7]

The British marched west to Concord. A mile from the farm that belonged to Colonel Barrett is the North Bridge which arches over the Concord River. This was where the colonials first fired on the British—"the shot heard 'round the world." Surprised British Regulars fell back and tried to escape to Boston, but many died retreating on what is now known as Battle Road, where Paul Revere was captured.

The area is now Minuteman National Historical Park and was the patriotic portion of our trip. Minuteman park rangers guided us through this history of Lexington and Concord. Through a multimedia presentation, a patriot led us into the tense moments when he and his neighbors vowed to stand their ground and save their homes. Each year on April 19th, the battle is reenacted, lest we forget.

Linda: The next town on our agenda was Walpole, New Hampshire. We departed Bedford, in Boston's busy airspace, winging our way to Lebanon, New Hampshire, the northernmost point of our tour. The rolling terrain of the White Mountains bright with fall color is beautiful when viewed at low altitude below a broken cloud deck.

We made it to our initial descent point in less than an hour. Over a ridge, the crossing runway came into view first. We had to get around another hill before we could see the one on which we were cleared to land. The air was bumpy as we

---

[7] https://en.wikipedia.org/wiki/Prince_Estabrook

swooped around the hill on final approach and settled onto the asphalt.

An employee greeted us with a smile, keys to a rental car, and a bottle of New Hampshire maple syrup, saying, "It's better than that stuff you get in Vermont—over there they paint their leaves."

On a road map, he pointed out places of interest along the way. "Don't miss the longest usable covered bridge in America." We checked it out, crossing the Connecticut River to Vermont and back to New Hampshire in minutes. Although it was practical back in the day to cover those old wooden bridges to keep them from collapsing under heavy winter snows, today we adore the nostalgic remnants of a romantic Currier & Ives era.

Mike: Nestled among the rolling hills of the Connecticut River Valley in southwest New Hampshire is the Inn at Valley Farms, a hundred-and-five–acre organic farm with a bed and breakfast. Innkeeper Jackie Caserta showed us to our cozy room in her restored 1774 Colonial home.

Jackie suggested we visit the headquarters of the world-famous Burdick's Chocolates there in tiny, quaint Walpole. We started with dinner at The Restaurant at Burdick's. The café is housed in a long, two-story white clapboard building built in 1800. Large windows overlook the main street of Walpole.

Outside seating is available on the full-length covered porch. Inside, twenty-five tables are quickly claimed, making advance reservations a good idea. Here we would have another gourmet experience: traditional French cuisine.

On the menu were such specialties as Cod Bonne Femme, Orchiette, and Monkfish Provençal. I started with one of my favorites, French onion soup. Linda considered Quiche Lorraine but chose Beef Stew Provençal instead. Afterward, a visit to the candy counter introduced us to Burdick's signature chocolate mice. They told us it takes three days to handcraft these whimsical creatures that melt in your mouth.

Back at Jackie's place, we stepped softly across the aged dark wood floor planks and snuggled under a generously thick comforter. In the morning, our hostess treated us to a three-course candlelight farm-to-table breakfast that would outdo anything else we would have on this trip, even at Massachusetts' famous Red Lion Inn.

She introduced us to popovers, fed us the freshest, yellowest eggs we'd ever had, and served us a fancy concoction of pear with maple. No wonder *Yankee Magazine* awarded this inn the 2010 Editor's Pick in "Best of New England." It must have been a lot of work to turn a defunct dairy farm into a dream destination. One night was not enough, and we vowed to return to the peaceful, romantic inn.

Linda: People in these small New England farming communities treat visitors nicely. We found New England pot pies, pumpkin ice cream, and maple-flavored everything in abundance in every town. Ice cream is quite popular in the northeast. I thought back to our honeymoon in Maine, where it seemed there was a locally owned ice cream store on every corner.

I still laugh at the memory of the moment I remarked to Mike, "There sure are a lot of ice cream shops here." Those words had barely passed my lips when we passed a building with the sign, "Don's Radiator Shop…and ice cream."

For several months, we researched and planned our fall foliage flying tour. One place that piqued our interest was the town of Weston, Vermont, described by a travel resource as being like a Norman Rockwell painting.

Through the Green Mountains on our way to Weston, we traveled country roads draped in old train trellises, past old houses mirrored by serene lakes as the fog finished its whisper to canoes waiting mostly on the shores, and the water smiled from ringlets of raindrops. Even with the apparent age of these places, splashes of fall color and a Maple Lane in every town sets the stage for great sightseeing.

Weston is home to the Vermont Country Store, a popular attraction for shoppers. Adorned with autumn-ness, the store's pumpkin-lined slate rock walkways accented by wood and iron benches and old wooden barrels, and dotted with mounds of bursting fall chrysanthemums, led to a welcoming porch with waiting rockers.

In the grass, set artistically off to the side of the porch, were a 1950s Chevy pickup and an old milk can. It was touristy-picturesque. Inside, a trip down memory lane in the candy department took me back in time with rock candy, jawbreakers, and yardstick bubble gum. We stayed one night in Weston; there was more of Vermont to see.

After lunch in Woodstock the next day, we roamed through an art gallery and a used bookstore, waiting for more flyable weather.

The bookshop was a cozy place to meander and held a surprise gift for my mom. She had just told me of a book about

Indians she wanted to find, written in the eighteenth century. Even after an exhaustive search online, the lowest price I could find reflected the rarity of the book—around twelve thousand dollars. When I asked the clerk where the Native American section was, he pointed to the corner and said, "If I have anything, it will be in a pile on the floor over there. I haven't gone through any of that."

It seemed such a long shot, yet when I sifted through the pile, there was the one my mom was looking for, covered in the stack on the floor. The sticker said fifteen dollars. I didn't want to rejoice too loud in case that might cause the price to increase, so I quietly took the thousand-page piece of history to the counter and calmly said, "This one will do." The clerk didn't know how excited my mom would be to have this book, or how happy I was by this find.

As the clouds cleared enough to make our next flight, we hurried back to the airport in Lebanon, New Hampshire.

Next stop: Stockbridge, Massachusetts, landing at the closest airport in nearby Pittsfield. It was my leg to fly on this "interesting" weather day. Light rain, but visibility was good. Still, a large band of low clouds meant a longer flight to find gaps where we could clear the mountains.

Since we don't have protection against icing, we would not fly in the clouds, as the temperatures would be below freezing. Pittsfield's airport was hiding behind a mountain range, but eventually we came upon it. Fortunately, the swift wind was blowing straight down the runway.

Mike: The friendly lineman at the airport drove the rental car onto the ramp to meet us and helped secure the plane. Only minutes away, Stockbridge has been home to the Red Lion

Inn since 1773. The large and elegant hotel has an operating bird-cage elevator and is decorated with thousands of antiques. For a full nostalgic experience, the inn provides turndown service, including chocolates on your pillow and a booklet with three short bedtime stories, a unique and charming touch.

Norman Rockwell lived his last twenty-five years in Stockbridge. His studio was moved onto property shared with the museum that bears his name. Here are most of his original paintings and tear sheets of every *Saturday Evening Post* cover he created. He worked twelve hours a day, seven days a week, including holidays, for most of his life. We spent the day at the museum that honors the beloved artist who captured daily life in America for many decades of the last century.

Too soon, our vacation was nearing an end. Crossing all the mountain ranges again, bright hues of orange, red, and yellow covered the landscape like a soft knitted blanket. White church steeples in small towns bid a warm goodbye. The video camera got a lot of use.

The same tailwinds we enjoyed on the way up to New England were headwinds on the way back, considerably reducing ground speed and requiring more fuel stops. The first came three-and-a-half hours after departing Pittsfield. After clearing mountain ranges, we landed in Morgantown, West Virginia. The airport was quite busy, which we learned was due to a local college football game. The attendant fueled the plane, the airport restaurant fueled us, and we were airborne again.

Linda: Often when we're traveling during football season, we end up at an airport in a town hosting an important game.

Usually it's the college games which fill general aviation ramps with aircraft of the many alumni who fly in.

A fuel stop in Knoxville, Tennessee, proved to be like the one in Morgantown. A football game was going full tilt when we contacted Knoxville Approach Control. It was my turn in the left seat. The approach controller vectored us around the University of Tennessee Neyland Stadium so we could get a good view, which, if I was a football fan—I know; I'll dodge the tomatoes—would have thrilled me.

"Grumman Niner Fife Eight, how'd you like that view of the game?" the controller asked as we flew along the southeast edge of the stadium. The Volunteers were playing the Alabama Crimson Tide and we figured it must have been halftime, judging by the barrage of camera flashes below—undoubtedly a capacity crowd in the 102,455-seat venue. My honest response to the controller probably set me apart from everyone else in town. "Well, I'm not much of a football fan, but I sure love flying!"

His quick follow-up likely hid his real feelings, saying, "Well, either way, it's a great view," before excusing me to switch my radio frequency to the airport's control tower.

Mike: The airport ramp was packed. Jets, turboprops, and piston airplanes filled almost every parking spot. "You here for the game?" was the presumptuous question posed more like a statement of fact until we shocked the TAC Air staff when we replied, "No, just a fuel stop and overnight." They told us it was good we called ahead, that we were lucky to get the last hotel room in town. Fortunately, it was right across the highway with a restaurant next door.

Linda: We arrived home the next day at Ellington Airport, just as the sun was setting. Once the airplane was tucked in, we closed the hangar doors, marking the end of our fall foliage flying tour.

Skyway Gypsies

Mike: What do you get when you mix two pilots with a couple of unexpected days off in the middle of a work week not contaminated by rain and thunderstorms? An airway trip!

After quickly assessing where to go, we chose west and tossed a few things into bags. Soon the *Elyminator's* wheels were up and leaving Houston. We turned the nose to 290 degrees on the compass. The flatlands below changed shape and character. Low rolling hills followed by fractured ground led to rugged slopes off plateaus, opening into canyons in a volcanic landscape.

West of Plainview, where we stopped for fuel, stockyards with covered silage mounds dotted the prairie. As though the land was taking steps, its elevation gradually increased, bringing the ground closer to us until we climbed higher. From our lofty perch, we could see well ahead as we crossed the plains.

This is an area I know from the westerns I read by Louis L'Amour and Luke Short. I could picture L'Amour's characters, Orin and Tyrel Sackett, somewhere down there riding herd or hunting up trouble. How would it have been for those adventuresome souls as they inched across that ground?

As we crossed the lower ridges of the Rockies heading into the valley near Santa Fe, I pointed out the Pecos River and all the lands in Lincoln County. That's where Billy the Kid rode and the Lincoln County War took place. We had climbed to over ten thousand feet alongside the snowcapped Truchas and other peaks.

Here, we swung north, hugging the west side of the Sangre de Cristo Range and traversed the reservations Tony Hillerman depicted in his Jim Chee novels. The polite, neighborly way to fly over the Indian reservations is to climb to 12,500 feet through the mountain passes. But with the wind howling through them and churning over the ridges, we took the long way around. Destination: Taos.

Linda: Unplanned adventures give us some of the best stories. This impromptu trip goes down as a win.

An airport is a community's front door, and an airport manager is often a transient pilot's first impression of a town; Taos didn't disappoint. The airport manager, Kino, offered a warm, friendly welcome to Taos and helped us arrange transportation and a place to stay. We had about twenty-four hours to explore the town.

The crew at the Don Fernando Hotel checked us in to a clean, modern, spacious room, at the pilots' special rate. We dropped our bags in the room and dashed out for a quick bite. They would be rolling up the streets in a few hours.

We found the area to be cute and quaintly New Mexico. A few of the shops were too commercialized for our taste, but then we discovered the extraordinary artwork of an inimitable artist: Charles Collins. He's called a Taos Master and upon seeing his work, we understood why.

Mike: We were drawn by the unusual six-something-foot-tall sculpture outside his gallery and wooed in by our curiosity. His beginnings as a potter and sometimes painter took turns that included the physical work of bronze sculpture. His pieces are unlike anything you've seen before.

Artist Collins believed the vision for his unique work was from God, so he called the series of sculptures *Mastermind*. What he produced is so captivating and original that the governor of New Mexico declared a Charles Collins Day.

What we found inside were smaller-sized creations of the one that bid us come. Imagine three individual statue-like pieces, each about a foot-and-a-half tall, that when placed together like a puzzle, create a full sculpted face of someone you'll recognize. Each is a story, every piece as well as the whole, a person.

His first was the face of Abraham Lincoln. Pull apart the three pieces and look first at the statue that makes up the left side of his face. Turn it around to discover a Union soldier, the piece on the right, a Confederate soldier. Turn around the middle section to reveal the maquette of Hope, the central female figure with strength and courage keeping them together. He named it *Lincoln's Union*.

In the *Mastermind* sculptures that depict the faces of George Washington, Shakespeare, Beethoven, da Vinci, and Christ, women are the centerpiece, symbolizing, said Charles, the ones who hold it all together. The three pieces point directly to the affirmation of his faith, the Trinity of God.

Charles was not in his gallery often, and we were grateful to have stumbled upon a real treat visiting with him in the tourist off-season when he was much more available.

Linda: The striking pink and orange sunset saw shops to their close, leaving mostly restaurants as the only remaining busy places.

As we meandered along the sidewalks, pleasant sounds reached us, audio waves coming from inside one of the restaurants. Making our way toward the comfortable harmonies, we happened upon a quartet called Screen Door Porch. Now that's got to be the most fitting name for a group that plays soulful Americana, roots-rock, and country blues.

We found a small table on the patio where we could watch the musicians through full-length windows. Lovely sounds spilled out the open door. This was comfy, blue jeans kind of music that makes you think of lazy day gatherings—friends on the front porch, iced tea, lemonade, a few instruments, and a good time.

By nightfall, we'd been in town about four hours, yet we felt as though we'd experienced a full day. We'd have half the next day to explore Taos, including the home of frontiersman Kit Carson.

Our morning began with a walking tour along the avenues of old Taos, by art galleries and shops not yet open. On the other side of adobe walls, through an old wood portal, is the courtyard entrance to Kit Carson's home. Now a museum, the home honors the larger-than-life scout, one of the most effective Indian agents in U.S. history. Although he stood just over five feet tall, he was a mountain of a man in his contributions to westward expansion.

Kit and his wife, Josefa, raised seven children in the four-room house. When Native people traveling long distances passed through Taos, the Carsons invited them to pitch their tents and teepees in the courtyard. Touring the house and reading the family's history gave us more of a taste of Taos. Too soon, our play time was up, and it was time to windsurf back to Texas.

We flew the *Elyminator* up and away from the art, music, and history of Taos, over the deep chasm cut by the Rio Grande. When our shadow danced across Santa Fe, we took the wide gap between the Sangre de Cristos from the Sandia Mountains east of Albuquerque. The headwind we flew into yesterday turned into a bumpy tailwind rocketing us back to Houston with the eager anticipation of the next gypsy trip.

Landing on Memory Lane

Linda: "A mile of highway can take you a mile, but a mile of runway can take you anywhere." That's a phrase we often use because its message hits the bull's-eye. With full power, the airplane thrusts forward, up, and away. Ahead are places waiting to take me back to a time before mine.

On a return to my hometown of Indianapolis, I gathered up Mom and my sister Barbara, and we headed for a special place: Mattoon, Illinois, where Mom grew up. We could not have fit this trip into a weekend were it not for the runways dotting the landscape. If not for these landing strips, Mom, Barbara, and I would not have stood together on the old brick road in front of the house at 915 Wabash Avenue where Mom was born in the winter of 1933.

We would have missed hearing her stories of hopping up and down the front porch steps that were right before us and of playing with her bulldog in the backyard. Thanks to the runways here and there and in between, the three of us took this priceless trip down memory lane.

When she was three, Mom and her family moved a few blocks over from Wabash Avenue to a historic house, the grandest in town. Their new address was 1121 Charleston Avenue. Mom's recollection of moving day made each moment come alive as we walked down the same roads, taking in the same neighborhood. As she spoke, I could see a little girl busying herself while waiting for the movers. She told of rolled-up, room-sized rugs brought out to the sidewalk to be loaded into the truck. Her words created the picture of a wide-eyed tyke fascinated that she could walk atop the rolled rugs, discovering that everything can be moved from its familiar place.

The youngest of four children born within six years, she wasn't allowed to ride with the big kids in the moving truck, so she walked with the dog and the housekeeper, who she said were probably her best friends anyway. With them, she would find adventure in a new-to-them century-old mansion.

Among her vivid memories is one of a portrait of the builder and original owner of their new residence. The painting, which hung at the top of the stairs, was of such large dimensions that Mr. Hasbrouck's descendants had no room for it in their homes. My grandmother assured them it would be no problem for it to remain with the house he built circa 1836.

Mom didn't know his first name, but telling us how she'd say, "Hello, Mr. Hasbrouck!" as she passed by his portrait through the years brought a gleeful smile and a twinkle in her eye. I imagined a cute little imp dashing through her active life full of spunk and charm. Unfortunately, the house is no longer there.

We pushed on with our day, stopping by some of the same restaurants and stores she shopped at long ago. Memories she shared made it difficult to leave each place where the past still felt alive.

On Broadway Avenue is the Illinois Central train depot, where Amtrak frequents today. The 1917 brick building presented itself proudly. Its restored antique staircase of ten-foot-wide terrazzo steps handsomely courted the ornamental metal and wood handrail. Original twelve-foot-long, high-back birch benches seemed to sit in waiting for the wood-and-metal ticket window. This, Mom said, was where she walked to greet her daddy every Friday evening. A chemist and inventor in train technology, he rode the rails home after a long work week across the country. She walked with him again every Sunday evening to see him off.

On the depot's third floor, the Mattoon and Coles County Historical Society opened doors to more reminiscing. In the society's library, we found a sweet surprise when a volunteer handed us a local high school yearbook from Mom's senior year. We turned its pages to see photos of Mom in more clubs and activities than I could imagine having time for. We learned this book had belonged to one of her friends, Louise Owings, whose family owned the town drug store.

There, in Mom's handwriting, was her *farewell-best-wishes-happy-graduation* message to Louise, along with her signature and an arrow to one of Mom's many photos. At first, Mom didn't suspect that it was her writing, and she snickered at the message: "Oh, how silly! Who wrote *that*!?" When I told her that was her signature, she was amused because she had to own up to it. The three of us roared with laughter at her realization. The volunteer was spot-on when she remarked, "That right there made the trip worth it."

I had launched from Baytown, Texas, and flown above countryside and towns to Midwestern cornfields where I found treasure buried deep in stories that sparkled to life as we stood in the places of Mom's memories. Those miles of runway have made possible journeys that have borne out many stories, like this one.

Then and Now

When I returned home, I longed to know more about the house on Charleston Avenue that sheltered my mom. I wanted to know about the doors she passed through to get to the next adventure. I wished my fingers could touch the walls that absorbed or echoed her chatter. I fancied my feet feeling the floors she skipped on to dinner and tiptoed on to bed, the same floors she landed on when she sprang out of bed for breakfast. I longed to regard the roof that helped her feel secure.

It made me sad the house was gone. The place of her childhood was razed around 1954. A bank now occupies the property, the coffer's presence I resent. It would have meant so much to be in the spaces where she practiced her singing for church, shared secrets with her sisters, and giggled in games of hide-and-seek.

All I could do to see the home she loved was hunt the internet for photos. I started my quest by identifying the man whose portrait had hung at the top of the stairs. He was Abram Hasbrouck. There were pictures of him, but none of the house.

Curious whether there were any Hasbrouck descendants who might have pictures, I continued my pursuit and learned that Mr. and Mrs. Hasbrouck had eight children—among them, Helen. Helen became Mrs. Isaac Craig and had four daughters. In her later years, she moved back to the old house. By then, it was owned by her eldest daughter, Louise Craig

Neal, who took care of her until Helen Hasbrouck Craig passed away.

Mr. and Mrs. Neal also had four daughters, including Elizabeth, who became Mrs. John Cartmill. She raised her sons, John Craig Cartmill and Robert Hasbrouck Cartmill, in Tulsa. John passed at the age of ninety-one. As I read his obituary, my heart nearly melted at the serendipity:

> *Flying was his first love. He was one of the first to graduate from the Army Air Corps Combat Flying School in Lubbock, TX in 1942 and served in World War II as a Glider Pilot. Continuing his love for aviation as a member of the Tulsa Skyhawks for many years, he had a particular love for soaring and spent many delightful hours under the cumulus clouds of Oklahoma.*

Then I discovered his brother Robert had passed on a year before John:

> *...a graduate of the U.S. Naval Academy Annapolis, MD, and earned a PhD in meteorology from the University of Oklahoma. He served as an officer in the U.S. Navy and was a veteran of the Korean War. His broad work experience included engineering, hydrology, meteorology, teaching, and farming. After retiring from NASA's Earth Resources Laboratory, he wrote a book,* The Next Hundred Years ... Then and Now, *comparing predictions made at the beginning of the twentieth and twenty-first centuries.*

I clicked through the internet until I found Robert's book. On the cover is a tiny photo of the house his great-great-grandfather built at 1121 Charleston Avenue, Mattoon, Illinois.

A mile of runway can take us anywhere—even back in time, where a walk through my mom's childhood is now planted firmly in my soul.

All in a Day's Work

Pilots take no special joy in walking. Pilots like flying.

—Neil Armstrong

Santa's Helpers

Mike: Santa's helpers don't always dress in red velvety elfin-wear. Sometimes their attire is more of a bluish-purple or brown hue. December is the peak season for the elves of FedEx and UPS, forecasting delivery of hundreds of millions of packages each Christmas.

What a busy and challenging time of year this is for air freight operators and pilots. The work increases 60 percent over other times of the year, so companies hire seasonal labor to handle the package volume. About fifty thousand people work temporary jobs with UPS to help deliver or work in sort facilities such as Louisville, Kentucky, and Rockford, Illinois. FedEx's seasonal work means lots of jobs in Memphis, Tennessee.

Their company jets will fly all those gifts from regional distribution and sort centers in major cities to hub cities. Then they'll transfer those presents to other cargo planes as "feeders" bound for smaller towns. Eventually, drivers will haul them in trucks to their destinations underneath Christmas trees across the country.

Pilots on the feeder routes fly a split morning and evening shift, making their way from the regional hub through several stops, arriving at the outstation by mid-morning. In the evening, the crews hopscotch back to the regional hub. Loaders transfer the packages onto bigger jets departing for the major sort centers.

During the three months leading up to Christmas, Santa's pilots log a lot of flight time while moving the excess volume. By the time Christmas Eve rolls around, some freight pilots have pretty much maxed out on the number of hours they can legally fly for hire during the year.

The freight carriers try hard to deliver all packages labeled "Christmas" by Christmas Eve. One Christmas Eve, my fellow company pilots had reached their legal for-hire flying limit. To get the last presents delivered, we, the Learjet crew who were not timed out, had to fly into smaller airports where jets don't normally land, like Payson, Arizona.

That afternoon as we finished unloading the boxes, a local lawman stuck his head through the airplane's doorway. "Excuse me, but do you know how fast you were going when you landed?"

"We crossed the fence at 123 knots," I replied.

"Hmm, that's what my radar gun said, too." He'd been having coffee at the airport café when he heard us announce our arrival on the airport's radio frequency. He and his friends dashed out to clock us on approach with his radar gun.

"Well seein' as it's Christmas and you being Santa's helpers and all," he grinned, "I guess I'll let it slide this time."

We ended up back at the Phoenix airport late on Christmas Eve, exhausted from several weeks of intense flying schedules. After fifteen years of this, I can tell you that on Christmas Day, Santa isn't the only one settling down for a long winter's nap. Most of Santa's helpers do, too.

Inky and Stinky

Mike: It was a Monday morning about five o'clock. A pilot was loading an airplane with containers on the UPS ramp at Ontario Airport in California. Once her airplane was filled with boxes and bags, she took off for California's Central Valley. The unpressurized twin-engine turboprop, a Beech 99, climbed over the San Gabriel Mountains and flew across the Mojave Desert at 10,000 feet. Beyond the southern Sierra Nevadas, the pilot landed at Bakersfield to offload her cargo. As she opened the rear doors, an incredible stench greeted her and the UPS truck driver.

They discovered a foul-smelling package leaking on everything around it and through the floor panels. The rewards of an Alaska hunting trip would be left to someone's memories—someone who boxed up a bag of moose meat on ice, not dry ice but the wet kind.

The package had arrived in Ontario from Alaska aboard a UPS freightliner on a Friday afternoon. Its status as second-day air did not guarantee a delivery date or time, so it was held for the Monday morning Bakersfield flight. Perhaps there was an effort to pinch a penny. But failing to mark the box "perishable" and pay for overnight delivery meant the once-frozen package remained on Ontario's ramp Saturday and Sunday in 100-degree heat.

Flying in the unpressurized cargo compartment caused the bag of rotten, smelly water to expand like a balloon and leak. The pilot and a mechanic cleaned and deodorized the airplane as best they could, but without success. That is how the Beechcraft BE99 known as N12AK became known to the pilots who flew her as Stinky.

Stinky had a sister ship—N34AK. Less than two weeks after that incident, I was flying a newly acquired red-and-white turboprop which still sported the paint scheme of the previous operator, Air Kentucky. My route was from Ontario to Bakersfield, the same route *eau de moose meat* had taken. After landing, I opened the cargo doors and saw red, gooey stuff oozing down the sides of several packages. With no markings, the boxes lay on their side or upside down, and whatever was inside was anybody's guess.

Pulling aside one of twenty red-soaked boxes, the UPS driver and I opened it to find two loosely closed Tupperware containers of printer's ink. We determined ten gallons of the stuff was leaking everywhere, seeping into the airplane's subfloor and through joints in the outer skin.

I cleaned as much as I could reach, and the mechanics did their part, but hiding away in crevasses there always seemed to be more that would streak the outside of the airplane every time it flew through rain. With the red-and-white paint scheme, it wasn't so obvious. But after the airplane was repainted blue and white, a flight through rain made the streaks quite noticeable. That is how the Beechcraft BE99 registered as N34AK became known as Inky.

The tales of Inky and Stinky describe two minor, even comical incidents, but shipping undocumented hazardous material by air, whether knowingly or unknowingly, is no laughing matter. One of our pilots had to land off-route unexpectedly after becoming sick. Someone, hoping to fool the system, sent something prohibited from being shipped by air. Noxious fumes emanating from the unsealed package almost incapacitated the pilot before he could land. Take this old freight dog's plea and properly mark your packages—doing so could save lives.

Earthquake

Mike: All was quiet in the wee hours of Monday morning. Oakland Center Air Traffic Control was working two targets, both were our company airplanes. We had departed Metropolitan Oakland Airport for Burbank about forty-five minutes earlier.

The Piper Chieftain I was flying could make the trip in two hours. The plane had flown this route so many times, I think it knew the way better than I did. The other pilot, Chris, was flying a Beech 99 turboprop. At this point, he was about fifty miles in front of me. Our cargo was canceled checks.

I like to keep the cockpit lights low at night to enjoy the brilliance of the stars stretched across the sky. The Bay Area city lights had long since slid behind us, and now only the dark night and the low throbbing drone of the engines remained. The Chieftain's exhaust stacks glowed white-hot through the louvers in the engine cowlings.

The radio crackled to life. "Hey Mike, look at the sky," came Chris on our company frequency.

Across the horizon danced a wild array of blue-green flashes. "What's that?" I asked.

The Oakland Center controller handed Chris off to Los Angeles Center while I wondered about the unusual flashes in the sky. Moments later, Chris called back. "They've had a major earthquake in L.A.!"

Los Angeles Center is in the high desert at U.S. Air Force Plant 42 near Palmdale, California, a hundred miles from downtown Los Angeles. The flashes were probably electrical transformers blowing up. Not likely they were earthquake aurora, as that has rarely been seen.

"The landlines into L.A. are out. No one down there knows what's going on, except it's a massive one," Chris radioed as he flew on ahead and kept me informed. "Burbank has backup power for runway lights."

I continued over the mountains. In the hills ahead, near Six Flags Magic Mountain, north of the San Fernando Valley, I would normally see a carpet of lights. There was only darkness punctuated by glimpses of fire. I could no longer rely on city lights to define my route over mountainous terrain.

As I approached, the outline of runway lights appeared to float into view—emergency power lighting a single runway. Burbank Approach Control cleared me to land but cautioned that the tower had been evacuated, so I was on my own once I landed. Several small fires that lined San Fernando Road came clearly into view as I descended. The landing itself was uneventful.

With no taxiway lights available, I inched my way along the taxiway to the ramp, and my thoughts turned to my family and friends, who I later learned were all fine.

On January 17, 1994, I waited at the airport until it was light enough to avoid the widespread damage of the Northridge 6.7 magnitude quake on that quiet, early Monday morning that began like any other.

Spinning Prop Yarns

Mike: Covering a deserving victim's front yard with toilet paper takes some effort. To do a good T.P. job, you have to run around quietly enough not to wake the neighborhood dogs, all the while suppressing snickers over anticipated reactions. Plus, it takes arm muscle, good aim, and either luck or expertise at tossing toilet paper rolls to get those things to unravel through tall branches. Ideally, your tossing talent will send your ammo smoothly through the air, up and over trees, bushes, fences, and yard art. Grip it right, and it won't become a wobbly, intact chunk of a failure, embarrassing you right in front of your friends. It's hard work.

But two teen boys found an easier way to blanket their small town. With access to an airplane and a case of toilet paper, it's no surprise the wipes wisped right out the windows. Celebrating their high school graduation by flying a Cessna 172 in a covert night flight, one was the pilot, the other the bombardier.

Holding on to the first sheets, the bombardier flung the rolls one by one out into the airplane's slipstream. The force of air unraveled them. Unfurling tush tissue swirled in the turbulent air churned up by the propeller. The ends turned and overlapped, forming shapes like a cloverleaf or an oblong circle. Some fell free and gently floated down like streamers.

Once the 300-sheet rolls settled into a steady descent, the wind gave them a few final shoves until they came to rest on buildings and trees. I'll wager it looked like a giant snowflake spread over the city.

The pranksters landed and snuck back to enjoy their masterpiece.

Tossing toilet paper is tough. It's lightweight and the fact that it had to unroll made the likelihood of hitting the bull's-eye more difficult than if the pair had been dropping something more solid, perhaps even wet and slippery.

It may sound fishy, but there's another story that came my way thirty years ago from a pilot who flew for California's Fish and Game Department. I met him when I was a flight instructor in Long Beach, California. He flew the department's single-engine Cessna airplanes. His job was multi-faceted, including inventorying game, transporting personnel, shooting aerial photography, and searching for illegal poaching activity. His report about planting trout in the backcountry lakes and streams of the Sierra Nevada is my favorite.

Fish and Game pilots accomplished the task in a Beechcraft King Air with a belly pod, which is where the fish rode. The King Air would fly low over a lake and jettison the load from the pod, much like a "borate bomber" would unleash red-orange slurry on a forest fire. Frequent fish flying made these pilots pretty good at the game—the piles of plummeting pesce almost always plopped down right on target. But in mountainous terrain, unpredictable air currents and turbulence can interfere with the pilot's aim.

On one such occasion, the pilot missed the small lake almost entirely. Normally, a game warden is on the ground in radio contact to ensure the drop zone is clear, as was the case on this day. Over the patch of water, the airplane's hatch opened a second too late. The payload flopped down on the shore, landing a short distance from a couple of startled fishermen who had no idea what was going on.

The addled anglers ran over to where the trout landed and gawked at *all those fish*. The game warden, seeing them in the middle of the "catch," couldn't resist the opportunity presented by this scene. He walked over and sized up the pile, looked at the men holding rods and reels, then looked back at the heap as he slowly removed his citation book from his pack.

The sportsmen protested, "No! A plane came by and dumped 'em here!"

"Right, sure," said the warden as he continued to cite the pair.

"Really! They just fell here, and we came over to look! You don't *really* think we caught all these, do you?"

"Yeah. They just fell from the sky," the warden baited them. They squirmed like a worm on a hook. But he couldn't keep from laughing at the flabbergasted fishermen, and soon the truth was out about the fishy downpour.

Pilot stories are often embellished and are known to fly off in comic directions. True or not, I love retelling such tall tales.

Tribute to Patriots

There are times when you devote yourself to a higher cause than personal safety.

– John Glenn

Allan Chambers' Letters Home

Allan Chambers was born in Liberty, Texas, in 1920. After graduating from Liberty High School, he attended Schreiner Institute in Kerrville. He became a flight instructor for the U.S. Army Air Corps and was honorably discharged in October 1944. Joining the China National Aviation Corp., he spent eighteen months flying Curtiss C-46s and Douglas C-47s in India and China. Allan flew nearly one hundred trips over "the Hump"—a difficult air route along the eastern Himalaya Mountains—an unprecedented and dangerous way to supply China during and after World War II.

With gratitude to his son, the Honorable Tommy Chambers, we have the distinction of sharing the following excerpts from letters Allan sent to his mother in Liberty during his time in India and China. We expect you'll relish *Allan Chambers' Letters Home* as much as we do. We recommend reading them out loud.

> *May 5, 1945, Karachi, India.* We left New York and went to Newfoundland, Azores, Casablanca, Tripoli, Cairo, Abadan, and here, Karachi, India. I saw Will Partlow for a few minutes in Cairo.
>
> *May 6, 1945, Calcutta, India.* Arrived here in Calcutta. It is a big place, but very dirty and hot. I received $100

pay in rupees, and it filled up my pockets. I went to church this morning.

May 8, 1945, Calcutta. We heard Germany surrendered, so today was declared a holiday.

May 12, 1945, Calcutta. You can sure see a lot of queer sights here. Everyone drives on the left side of the road and there are carts, horse carts, ox carts, and hand carts. They use brahma cattle and water buffalo to do work.

June 11, 1945, Dinjan, India. I have been flying with the Chinese fellow that brought Doolittle out of China.[8]

June 20, 1945, Dinjan. That big shot in China came down here yesterday, I won't attempt to spell his name but he's the President and everything else.[9]

July 20, 1945, Dinjan. I did quite a bit of flying this month. I put in 21 round trips. Some of the snow-capped mountains look like Colorado, except they are higher here. I am sorry to hear about Nolan and Glynn.[10] That is too bad.

July 22, 1945, Dinjan. We have to fly on a different type of airplane than we have been flying…got a hair-cut in a regular barbershop in town, it had chairs and electric clippers.

---

[8] Moon Fun Chin—a Chinese pilot who flew Lt. Colonel Jimmy Doolittle out of China after his aerial raid on Japan in 1942.

[9] Believed to be Generalissimo Chiang Kai-shek.

[10] Nolan Pickett and Glynn Miles, both from Liberty, were killed in World War II.

August 1, 1945, Dinjan. I am glad to hear the cattle are fat, and it seems like now would be a good time to sell some calves and all of the old cows. I am sorry for the Miles and the Picketts.

August 12, 1945, Calcutta. I hear the Japs are about to quit the war.

August 15, 1945, Calcutta. I just heard the war is over…since that new bomb came out, it must be a very powerful thing.

August 22, 1945, Calcutta. The war is over! But there's still a lot to do in China and Japan. I might quit flying the Hump but then again, I might not. I am flying a different type plane here in Calcutta.

August 29, 1945, Dinjan. I'm still flying the Hump, but I heard I might be moving to Shanghai. If I do move into China, I guess I'll be out of India altogether. There has not been a lot of changes made since the war is over. I hear Hong Kong and Shanghai were nice before the war, so maybe they'll be an improvement over Calcutta.

Sept. 6, 1945, Dinjan. I have been flying out of Dinjan which is in the Assam Valley of northern India. We made trips to Kunming and Luhsien, which is near Chungking. We see mountains that are 17,000, 18,000, and 20,000 ft. along the way.

Sept. 7, 1945, Dinjan. Even though the war is over there is still plenty of flying to be done.

Sept. 11, 1945, Dinjan. I got back up here to Dinjan on the 11th, and I made a trip to Kunming yesterday and will probably make one today.

Sept. 16, 1945, Dinjan. I have been flying the last few days and have been to Kunming two more times. I started to go to Canton and Hong Kong but did not go on that trip. Today was like fall in Kunming, cool and clear.

Sept. 23, 1945, Dinjan. From Kunming the other day I went up to a place called Hsichang, up in the mountains. One of our planes was stuck in the mud. That country is sure pretty when you are on the ground. The little airport is just a green field 5,000′ above sea level. On all sides there are 12–14,000 ft. mountains. They look straight up when you are down in this valley. The U.S. is sure putting a lot of money into China.

Sept. 27, 1945, Kunming, China. I am here in Kunming and make about a trip a day over the Hump to Dinjan and back. The weather has been pretty good on the Hump.

Oct. 3, 1945, Kunming. I am staying here in Kunming and flying to Dinjan. Two different government groups are fighting in town, there will probably be a lot of trouble in China before long. I might quit flying the Hump at the end of this month and move to Shanghai.

Oct. 8, 1945, Dinjan. Yesterday we took a load of money to Luhsien. It was about $100 million. Now we are hauling gasoline, steel, some money, and radio and medical supplies. While the war was on, we hauled gasoline, shells, powder, dynamite, steel, and bales of cotton. We fly C-46's and C-47's. The C-46 is a bigger plane.

Oct. 18, 1945, Calcutta. I am back in Calcutta today. I came all the way from Shanghai in one day. It was 13½ hours flying time with stops in Kunming and Dinjan. The Hump flying may be over soon.

Oct. 25, 1945, Dinjan. I have been flying nearly every day. Dinjan is in a valley surrounded by mountains that usually have clouds on them.

Nov. 8, 1945, Calcutta. My new job is flight instructor. We have Chinese students and they don't understand English.

Nov. 15, 1945, Calcutta. We are about finished flying the Hump. On the way down here, we flew over Myitkyina, Burma. There was a big fight for the city during the war and now there are only 2 or 3 buildings left.

Nov. 16, 1945, Calcutta. I have 3 students that I fly in the mornings. It looks like they're going to have a real civil war here in China. I sent Billie 20 yards of silk.

Dec. 2, 1945, Calcutta. Not much flying lately, our airplanes have had engine trouble. I can't find a rosary here. Thanksgiving was last Thursday, but it was just another day for me.

Dec. 19, 1945, Calcutta. I will probably be going to Shanghai the first of the year. It's cold up in China and the Japanese took all the heating systems out of the buildings.

Dec. 28, 1945, Calcutta. I'm through instructing and will be going up into China soon. This is an R.A.F. airfield and will soon be abandoned. There are millions of dollars of airplanes that are being destroyed, but I guess that's the only thing to do.

Jan. 24, 1946, Nanking, China. I have been all over China since I wrote last. Over to Chungking, Peiping[11], Hankow, and up to Tsingtao. I'm going to Chungking tomorrow, hauling gasoline and bringing people back. They crowd people in these planes like you would cattle in a boxcar! There are a lot of Japanese planes here that people are fixing up and flying.

Feb. 3, 1946, Nanking. I have been flying all over the country. I left Chungking yesterday and flew to Peiping and back to Nanking today. General Marshall was at my hotel in Peiping the last time I was there.

March 17, 1946, Shanghai, China. There is a world of business here in China. Since C.N.A.C. is a government organization they should to have the inside track.

March 23, 1946, Hankow, China. The weather is bad, cold, rainy, muddy. I'm going on my way to Nanking.

April 28, 1946, Shanghai. We have been moving equipment out of Kunming. We quit flying the Hump last week. My base pay is $800 a month and up to $400 extra for overtime.

---

[11] Now Beijing; formerly Peiping and Peking.

May 5, 1946, Shanghai. I just got back from Chungking. The next time I go out it'll probably be for a couple of weeks.

May 31, 1946, Shanghai. I haven't flown for a week because everybody's on strike. We quit flying the Hump about a month ago, I was high enough on the pilots list that I wasn't sent down there. I got about a hundred trips over the Hump when I was there. The civil war is still going on in North China. Anything can be bought on the black market.

June 7, 1946, Shanghai. The Chinese Air Force took over the airline. Now we have about 3 ships flying a day and the Chinese Air Force flies 3 or 4.

June 27, 1946, Shanghai. There is supposed to be a truce on the Civil War, but I think both sides break it each day. People all over the world never had it so good as when the U.S. Army & Navy were there, or any Americans. I will probably go to Chungking or Hong Kong tomorrow.

July 12, 1946, Shanghai, I think I'm going to Hong Kong tomorrow. We are about finished moving the government to Nanking. I should be getting a $200 a month increase in pay.

July 23, 1946, Shanghai. We are getting men from the U.S. every month. We have about 75 planes now and supposed to get 6 new ones next month. I am going to Hong Kong tomorrow.

August 3, 1946, Shanghai. It's hot here, but not as hot as Calcutta. I'm supposed to go to Chungking tomorrow and be back the next day. The civil war is still going on.

August 16, 1946, Shanghai. We are flying passengers now like a regular airline. I flew to Kuling the other day, that is where all the big shots spend the summer months in China.

Sept. 27, 1946, Shanghai. I am flying C-46's and C-47's and am carrying passengers to Chungking, Canton, Hong Kong, Hankow, Nanking, Tsingtao, and Peiping. Summer is over.

Oct. 16, 1946, Shanghai. I have transportation on the S.S. Marine Lynx to leave tomorrow for San Francisco by way of Hong Kong and Manila. The shipping company said they had an extra ticket. I better take it because it is a lot of trouble to get out of China.

Allan Chambers arrived in San Francisco in November 1946. His wife, Billie, met him there. They returned to Liberty where they lived, until his death in 1996, in the house his grandfather built.

J.P. and the Collings Foundation

The Seat Still Fits

Mike: His Texas A&M cap and a beaming smile were all I could see. "It still fits, can you believe that?" As his attention turned back to the instruments, I knew his hands were finding the controls and his feet the rudder pedals. For J.P. Greenwalt, who was in his seventies, sitting in the cockpit of an F-100 Super Sabre was like a time warp back to his twenties.

The *Elyminator* was undergoing an annual inspection in our hangar at Ellington Airport. Our neighbors directly across the ramp had a few interesting pieces of history, so I invited J.P. to come out and look around. Dropping the kitchen remodeling project, he donned that A&M cap and dashed over with three cameras strapped carefully around his shoulders and torso like little papooses. After surveying our airplane in its undressed state, we walked over to see the folks at the Collings Foundation.

A non-profit organization, the Collings Foundation maintains retired military aircraft in airworthy condition in several locations. For historical education, they fly their collection in air shows and air tours around the country. At Ellington, they've kept a Lockheed T-33 Shooting Star jet trainer, a Douglas A-4 Skyhawk carrier-based attack aircraft, a Bell UH-

1 (Huey), the North American F-100, and a McDonnell Douglas F-4 Phantom. They also have a World War II Messerschmitt Me-262 jet fighter.

When the hangar doors were open, the *Elyminator* faced nose-to-nose with the F-100, the United States' first fighter capable of supersonic speeds in level flight. I think Linda wished that daily faceoff would make the *Elyminator* go faster, like maybe she could harness a little of that speed.

I left J.P. in the hands of Alan Arrowood, the guy who kept these airplanes flying, and went back to our hangar to work with our mechanic. When I returned, I found J.P. sitting high in the cockpit reliving his days as a pilot with the 119th Fighter Squadron, Tactical Fighter Group, New Jersey Air National Guard in Atlantic City. He carries a faded photo in his wallet of him in his younger days, wearing his flight suit and looking dapper in front of his trusty Super Sabre. I snapped another picture of him so he can show everyone how little things have changed.

J.P. had been talking about ejection seats when Alan smiled and said, "I love the look on their faces when they see these planes. They just light up the world. It takes them back to a different time and place. That's one of the reasons I do this job."

J.P. moved from the military into the airlines, flying for TWA, which eventually merged with American Airlines. He decided that over thirty years of airline flying was enough and retired as a captain on the Lockheed L-1011 wide-body jetliner. He doesn't fly anymore unless he gets a chance to jump into the cockpit of an F-100 and fly back in time.

Leadership

Mike: A U.S. Navy Corsair strafes a beach in North Korea. Back and forth, in each turn, the pilot's muscles tense as he pulls the control stick tight against his belly. He raises the nose high, banks left, and stomps hard on the left rudder. Reversing his course and diving, blood rushes from his head due to increasing G-forces. The long stretch of sand slides back into view. He levels out going nearly 400 miles an hour.

A U.S. Air Force F-86 smolders beside the dense trees and brush that choke the beach. The downed pilot has escaped to the ocean, so enemy soldiers shoot at him. Each time the Corsair storms the beach, its wing cannons belch fire in a deafening roar, ripping trails of splattering sand. The enemy scatters like a colony of ants whose mound has been disturbed. The airman surfaces for a breath before submerging again and swims farther out in the sea where a helicopter can rescue him.

"How long would you have stayed there covering him?" my dad asked.

Cousin Jack replied, "'Til I had enough fuel to get offshore a mile or two. Then I'd ditch. Luckily, I didn't have to, but that was the difference. They'd give up ten men to get one piece of equipment. We'd give up ten pieces of equipment to save one man."

Herman John "Jack" Trum III wanted to fly, but he also wanted to sail the seven seas. What do you do if you want to do both? Join the Navy. Jack won a cadet slot at the United States Naval Academy, Annapolis, Class of 1940. He was nine years older than my dad. Each was an only child. In their youth, Dad looked up to Jack like a young boy does an older brother. Jack watched over Dad, helped him with things like math homework when he was around, and called to talk when he wasn't.

After graduation, Jack served as a midshipman on a battleship in the North Atlantic. Their secret mission was to find and "use any means necessary" to sink the German battleship *Tirpitz,* sister ship to the *Bismarck.* Unknown to them, at the time of the December 7 attack on Pearl Harbor, the ship had already been sunk. Jack went on to flight training, finishing World War II as a Naval Aviator. He was one of the few of his graduating class to survive the war.

During the Korean War, Jack flew as a squadron commander for 104 missions. He told of flying so low at times that upon returning to the ship, mud had to be washed from the plane's belly.

His career progressed from fighter squadron commander to fleet oiler captain and then captain of the aircraft carrier *USS Oriskany.* He was promoted to Rear Admiral in 1967, serving on two carrier divisions. His final appointment was Commandant of Naval Air Station Whidbey Island in Washington, where he retired in 1972.

In adulthood, the reunion of Dad and Jack was an annual event. They would pick a city, tour it together, and share a weekend like brothers. I'm sure many of the old stories were repeated several times.

During one such reunion, right after the Navy's Tailhook scandal ended the careers of the Chief of Naval Operations and Secretary of the Navy, Dad asked Jack if he thought the punishment was too severe.[12]

Jack replied, "It wasn't severe enough. They either knew or should have known what's happening during their watch. Neglecting their responsibilities is not the quality of a leader. There is no gray area."

We lost both Dad and Cousin Jack years ago, but their influences remain. Jack's words instilled integrity and have helped me when facing difficult decisions. In him, I saw leadership.

---

[12] https://en.wikipedia.org/wiki/Tailhook_scandal

The Grandfather: Lawrence Dewey Bonbrake, Airplane Designer and Builder

Lawrence Dewey Bonbrake was born in the right place, at the right time—Woodston, Kansas, 1899. The industrial revolution had spurred new ideas, and the gasoline-powered automobile nearly shared Dewey's date of birth. Mechanical wonders drew the world's fascination and fueled the imagination of a youngster who liked tinkering with projects that exercised his mind and hands.

Twelve-year-old Woodston boys like Dewey must have heard the buzz from halfway across the state and felt the spirit of adventure the day an airplane first flew in Kansas.[13] They would get to see one of those flying machines in person the next year, when an aviator flew into town offering rides.

Imagine how the sounds of an approaching airplane electrified them. They heard the clicking of the engine's valve lifters, its propeller at full throttle like playing cards in their bicycle spokes. Then, as the aviator reduced power to descend, they were lulled by the whine of air flowing around singing wires and struts that held the machine together. They gawked

[13] September 2, 1911, Albin K. Longren became the first to build and fly an airplane in Kansas. http://cjonline.com/stories/090301/kan_history.shtml#.WcqERHaGPIU

in wonder as the plane crossed over a line of trees and landed in a farmer's field. Dewey would fancy himself in that cockpit, looking through oil-stained goggles toward the sun setting over a distant horizon. Oh, how he wanted to fly!

Increasing news of flying machines inspired Dewey and his cousin to build a glider. With ropes and pulleys, they lifted it carefully to the roof of their barn to put it to the ultimate test. They did it! Their glider drifted gracefully and settled onto the ground in one piece. Such a victory brought encouragement for more projects, like the sled to which Dewey attached a motorcycle engine and a propeller. When he rode it nineteen miles to the next town, Stockton, someone wrote an article about the fifteen-year-old kid with a powered sled. Dewey was absorbed in his mechanical discoveries. Around the world, the speed of invention seemed to be at full throttle, as did the First World War. If he was going to build airplanes, the next logical step was college.

Dewey chose Valparaiso University in Indiana to study engineering. With a singular focus, his doodles became sketches, which grew into drawings. By the time he was nineteen, he had designed a single-pilot air ambulance.[14] His plans could have helped the war effort, but the Armistice came later that year. Even so, a flying ambulance could serve civilians in peacetime, an idea that wouldn't take hold for another decade.

When the war ended, the government was eager to sell their fleet of training aircraft, the Curtiss Jenny. Prices were as low as $200. Men and women seeking adventure saw an opportunity, and civilians were soon taking to the sky. Dewey

---

[14] Dewey used a Liberty engine for his air ambulance.

acquired one, too, and became a barnstormer, just like the fellow who flew into Woodston when Dewey was thirteen. No imagination needed. He was now that pilot looking through oil-stained goggles toward the setting sun on a distant horizon.

Lawrence Dewey Bonbrake with Curtiss JN-4 Jenny, 1920

Barnstorming burgeoned as popular entertainment, like a circus coming to town. Pilots performed aerial stunts, sometimes as part of a group—a flying circus—although many traveled solo. Across the country, they would find a town, fly low at full throttle just above Main Street to get attention, and land nearby. They stayed a few days, selling airplane rides and performing stunts before moving on to the next town.

Life as an aerial gypsy was living on the edge, which Dewey found out doesn't leave much room for mistakes. One time, while flying his Jenny across Arizona, Dewey ran out of gas and landed in the desert. The danger of heat stroke, or worse, was thwarted thanks to a stranger passing through on a donkey cart. Nothing more is known of the man who helped Dewey get gas for his airplane, although he thanked him before taking off, back into the sky.

Another time, a man who bought a ride claimed to be a pilot. He must have been persuasive because Dewey let him have the pilot's seat, which is the rear seat. Dewey took the front, where he had removed the control stick so passengers could not interfere with a flight. Unfortunately, the so-called pilot got the airplane into a flat spin—a very dangerous situation—and there was nothing Dewey could do to stop it. The family story goes that to prepare for the crash, with the world spinning 'round, Dewey gave himself up to his fate. He removed his goggles, put them in his pocket, and waited for the inevitable.

When help arrived, Dewey was unconscious, and his face mangled. His upper lip had been cut off, top front teeth knocked out, and his nose and cheekbones were broken. Rescuers found the passenger moving and took him to the hospital, but left Dewey for dead.

He wasn't dead, and eventually his wounds healed, but the other guy wasn't so lucky. He had more extensive injuries, perhaps internal. He succumbed in the hospital.

Despite the accident, barnstorming wasn't a bad gig. Most important for Dewey, it led to meeting his future wife. Traveling town to town, he happened to walk into an ice cream shop in Kansas City, where the lovely Leona Alita Lamb had stopped in for a treat. She was the strong-willed daughter of prominent saddle maker Willie Lamb of Arkansas. Dewey, the handsome young man all dressed out in his jodhpurs, helmet, and goggles, was determined to marry her.

Leona Lamb Bonbrake with Dewey's Curtis JN-4 Jenny, 1921

Since her teens, she had been the mother figure for her eight siblings after their mother died suddenly from a gallbladder infection. The clever, tenacious woman she became made her a good accomplice for Dewey. After they wed, friends and family bestowed on her the affectionate nickname, "General Bonbrake."

The "General" wasn't over five feet tall. She was neat, but not flashy, intelligent, and well-dressed. Her handwriting was exuberant, precise, and beautiful—her letters large, as she was in the lives of those who knew her. She encouraged Dewey and helped him make important career connections, like the one that led to bringing his airplane designs to market, starting with the Parasol.

Dewey and his friend Bert Thomas had bought a Bahl Lark monoplane but discovered it was a terrible flying airplane. They redesigned it and named it the Bonbrake Parasol.[15] Dewey showed the prototype to potential investors, hoping to find the best financial backing and put the airplane into production. Leona's philosophy was to start at the top.

There wasn't much higher to go than Samuel Insull, an English immigrant living in Chicago. He was one of the most powerful merchants in U.S. history, a tycoon who once served as the personal secretary to Thomas Edison and was a founder of Edison General Electric. Dewey's connection was Arthur Hardgrave, a pilot and businessman who worked for some of

---

[15] The Bahl Lark was a single-seat parasol with a three-cylinder engine designed by Errold Bahl and made in Nebraska. The fuselage hangs below a single wing, attached by struts and flying wires. Bahl was mentor to Charles Lindbergh before Lindbergh had his pilot certificate.

While Bahl was barnstorming, Lindbergh served as his mechanic and wing-walker. https://en.wikipedia.org/wiki/Barnstorming. The prototype for his new airplane design improved upon the Bahl Lark and used the 40-horsepower French Anzani engine off the Lark. http://www.aerofiles.com/tuxhorn-text.jpg.

the Insull companies.[16] When Samuel Insull invested in Dewey's dream, the Bonbrake Parasol was renamed the Inland and went into production. Inland Aviation opened for business in 1928 at the Fairfax Airport in Kansas City.[17]

The National Air Races and Aviation Exhibition in Los Angeles offered the best opportunity for inventors and manufacturers to unveil new ideas to the budding aviation industry. Arthur Hardgrave and Tom "Gene" Gabbert, an engineer and test pilot, flew the Inland prototype to the event.[18] There they introduced Dewey's creation to the who's who of the flying world. Next, they would have to validate their assertion that they could build a superior flying machine. They set their sights on attaining altitude and speed records.[19]

---

[16] Hardgrave was president of City Ice and served as president of the Kansas City Chamber of Commerce, and the Rancho De La Osa Guest Ranch outside Tucson. On the way from Kansas City to Los Angeles, they landed at Davis-Monthan in Tucson, the first municipal aviation field in the U.S. The Davis-Monthan historic register recorded airplanes that landed there, their pilots and passengers, between 1925 and 1936. Gene Gabbert and Arthur Hardgrave signed it the morning of September 5, 1928. According to https://dmairfield.com/, the register records seven landings by six different Inlands. The website offers a good narrative on each of the Inlands listed. Their next stop was the Guest Ranch.

[17] In 1928 the Inland Sport was built in the same building as the Rearwin and American Eagle. Inland Aviation announced its first commercial airplane in September 1929 in *Aviation Magazine* and other publications.

[18] Gene Gabbert was a test pilot for Unit Motors and Airplane Co., Kansas City, MO.

[19] Records were set in the Inland in 1929 and 1930. The airplane reached 19,000 feet, breaking the previous record of 18,000 feet and with only a 110-horsepower engine. They also set a record of 125 miles an hour on a closed course.

The airplane placed well in races around the country. During the 1930 National Air Race in Chicago, Arthur Hardgrave captured first place in an Inland. Inlands also took second and third. Female pilots Mae Haizlip, Vera Dawn Walker, and Martie Bowman celebrated top finishes flying Inlands in several other major air races.[20] These victories proved their product.

Samuel Insull's business success helped Dewey pursue his ambition until the third year of the Great Depression. When the Insull dynasty went bankrupt in 1932, so did Inland Aviation, putting the brakes on all that Dewey Bonbrake worked so hard to build.[21]

The firm had produced dozens of airplanes, and while the exact number is not known, Dewey's grandson, Lance Borden, estimated forty-six. Only four were registered with the FAA as of 2019.

---

[20] Arthur Hardgrave won first place in the Sportsman class followed by Inlands in second and third place. Mae Haizlip, Vera Dawn Walker, and Martie Bowman flew Inland Sports. By this time, they had three models: the Sport, a 70-horsepower LeBlond, a five-cylinder radial which sold for $3,500, the Sportster, a 90-horsepower, five-cylinder Warner Scarab engine offered for $3,700, and the Super Sport, a 125-horsepower Warner Scarab seven-cylinder radial with a price tag of $4,500.

[21] "Emergence of Electrical Utilities in America," Smithsonian Institution, National Museum of American History.
http://americanhistory.si.edu/powering/past/h1main.htm.
House of Morgan spread rumors in order to sink the stock value, and then took control of Samuel's holding company. "Samuel Insull: Getting the Story Straight," James L. Johnston. https://www.heartland.org/news-opinion/news/samuel-insull-getting-the-story-straight.

Lawrence Dewey Bonbrake, circa 1925

Following the company's demise, Dewey moved to Houston to work as a security guard for Shell Oil on the ship channel.[22] One day, an Inland Sportster flew over Dewey's house. He dashed out to follow it, hoping to meet the pilot.

Tracking the plane in his car, he turned down the road that led him to the landing spot. To his surprise, the pilot was a thirteen-year-old kid. Charlie Walling introduced himself and explained that he had convinced a couple of cops to teach him to fly. While others had turned him down for flight lessons

[22] Dewey still designed airplanes during and after the Depression. One he called the Osage, but he never built it.

when he was twelve, these guys at Houston's Main Street Airport agreed to teach him for five dollars an hour.[23] He'd recoup that money by teaching others to fly.

Inland Sport Prototype

Dewey felt a kindred spirit in Charlie Walling, despite their twenty-two-year age difference. They swapped stories of inspiration and experimentation and compared how each had been enthralled with flight as a youngster. Dewey liked that Charlie had been influenced at the age of five by Charles Lindbergh's solo flight across the Atlantic Ocean. It seemed to frame their friendship well. Lindbergh had been mentored by Errold Bahl, whose airplane design Dewey perfected to become the Inland and which Charlie bought from the cops for $200.

[23] Any trace of that airport is now covered by houses, north of the intersection of Interstate 610 and Main Street, less than a mile west of the Astrodome. http://www.airfields-freeman.com/TX/Airfields_TX_HoustonS.htm#maintst

Lawrence Dewey Bonbrake with Inland, 1929

Dewey and Charlie got along famously. The elder friend hosted the kid at his home often where a small group of aviation enthusiasts gathered to build model planes. The boy pilot would grow up to fly during World War II, over the Hump of Burma. He would later race a P-51 at the National Air Races and retire as a corporate pilot in Houston.

After several years in Houston, Dewey moved to Los Angeles to join Lockheed and Consolidated as a designer on the Constellation project, the airliner built at the request of Howard Hughes. In his career, he contributed to several other aircraft manufacturers, helping with the development of many more important flying machines, including Boeing's B-36.[24]

In 1944, Dewey had a short stint in Los Alamos with the University of Southern California. He served as a chief engi-

---

[24] Dewey worked for Vultee, Consolidated, and Lockheed again, and then Fairchild. He also worked on the designs of the Electra P-3, Pogo, and C-130, followed by the Fairchild F-27 and C-119.

neer on the "Manhattan Project," code name for the secret development of the atomic bomb. He and his team designed the trigger mechanism.[25]

Exposure to radiation gave Dewey skin cancer, but it was severe nosebleeds which caused him to return to Los Angeles after only a few months. Los Alamos' elevation is about 7,000 feet above sea level. His family believed his facial injuries from the crash were likely to blame for his altitude intolerance. These days, they look back to that distant horizon and remember the kid with the powered sled—oh, how he'd wanted to fly! He did that and more. His was a life well lived, weathering storms along the way with Leona "General" Bonbrake ever present at his side.

Photos courtesy Lance Borden, from family photo albums.

---

[25] Dewey was a chief engineer in the Ordnance and Engineering Division. https://history.aip.org/phn/manhattan-project.html#losalamos1

The Grandson: Lance Borden, Radio Man

** Contains some graphic description of war*

Lance Borden owned one of the few surviving Inland airplanes, a Super Sport model, designed by his grandfather, Dewey Bonbrake. He's proud of the rare airplane's history, and of his beloved grandfather, whom he called "Gaga."

Grandfather's Radio

While their dad was serving as an electrical engineer in the U.S. Air Force in Korea, Dewey was a strong influence for Lance and his older brother Jim. When Lance was seven, Gaga bought a Philmore crystal radio for Jim. The boys were fascinated watching their grandfather hook it up. WSB radio, broadcasting from the Biltmore Hotel, was the only station they could pick up in 1953 Atlanta. Jim would take the earphones off his headset and hand one to Lance. Together, the brothers listened to radio programs like *The Kitchen Klub* and *It Pays to Listen.*

Lance stared at the crystal as they lay in their beds, stealth words wafting to his ears. His inquisitive mind pondered. *How does that work? How do those sounds come off the air and hit that wire? What's magic about that to make a radio, so I can hear all this?* It was an enchanting mystery he would later learn.

When their dad returned from Korea, Lance persisted for an explanation of the magic. He was too young to comprehend it all, although Gaga had tried to help. He couldn't quite grasp his dad's answer either, but Jim was seventeen and understood the concepts. Their dad saw the potential for Jim to go into business, so he set up a radio and TV shop in their basement. He hired a couple of technicians to fix the radios and called the business Jimmy's TV and Radio Repair.

Lance kept after his dad, the repairmen, and his brother, insisting they teach him about radio. His dad did his best to describe rectification and electronics so that Lance would see it was science and not magic.

Inspiration

Gaga Bonbrake passed away when Lance was nine, but his memories continued to inspire. Lance had seen the model for his grandfather's Inland and heard stories about the airplane that fueled his interest. Like his grandfather, at age fifteen, Lance built a hang glider from bamboo, plastic, and things he bought at the hardware store. Recalling that time makes him laugh: "It even flew a hundred feet or so."

He and Jim had already tried jumping off their parents' two-story house using bed sheets as a parachute, which Lance concedes, "It's a good thing we didn't take the hang glider off the house!"

Maybe his love of flying also had something to do with his first airplane ride at fifteen, in an Aeronca Champ. The owner offered to sell it for $800. Lance mowed lawns trying to earn enough money to buy it, but $800 was a lot of money for a kid in 1961. Airplane ownership would have to wait.

A Change in Course

Lance planned to enter Ohio State University as a pre-med student, but after a summer spent on a fishing boat in Cape Hatteras, North Carolina, he returned too late to start classes. This led to receiving a draft notice from the Army, which caused him to enlist in the Air Force.

His passion for airplanes and electronics forged his path in the service. In technical school at Keesler Air Force Base in Biloxi, Mississippi, Lance learned how to repair aviation navigation aids. "Navaids" are ground-based equipment that transmit radio signals to receivers in aircraft that convert them into position and directional information displayed on the instruments in the cockpit.

After completing technical school, the Air Force assigned him to Carswell Air Force Base near Fort Worth. His job was to install and repair radio equipment on B-52 bombers and KC-135 aerial refueling Stratotankers.

While working at Carswell, a pivotal moment in the summer of 1968 would lead to a life-changing decision. Avionics technicians returning from Southeast Asia told Lance they received combat pay for shop work. The higher rate enticed him to volunteer. He applied for an assignment and received orders transferring him to the 432nd Combat Support Group, an F-4 Phantom unit at Udorn Air Force Base in northern Thailand.

Before shipping out, he was sent to Hamilton Air Force Base in California for crash courses in hand-to-hand combat tactics, knives, and guns. He wondered why an avionics tech would be put through such a course. He was even more puzzled when after the training, he was given a maroon diplomatic Embassy passport. Something felt out of place. Without a military passport, he would have no protection.

Arriving at Udorn, he sat in the Central Base Processing Office all day. At closing time, all the other guys had been processed except for Lance and another avionics tech from a B-52 base in Mississippi. He thought, *What a fine mess I've gotten myself into.*

Wondering about their future, they reminded the men in charge they had not been processed. But the men didn't register any concern and only responded, "We know."

As the last shade was drawn, a sergeant motioned to them and asked for their orders. When they handed them over, he folded them and placed them in a drawer, and pulled new orders from a different drawer. The two avionics techs were reassigned to Detachment 1, 56th Air Commando Wing at Udorn. They voiced their objections: "Hey, we're not air commandos; we are electronics guys." The processing sergeant repeated, "Yeah, I know."

An escort led them to a waiting area and told them their ride would be there shortly. A Jeep arrived five minutes later. Out hopped Sergeant Dennis, sporting bloused fatigues, jungle boots, and an Aussie hat, the brim folded up on one side with AIR COMMANDO emblazoned in large black letters. He was an easily likeable guy.

Sergeant Dennis was in charge of the radio shop. Riding in the Jeep that first day in Udorn, past the CIA's Air America ramp, Lance and the other tech could only imagine why they were there and what their assignment would be. On the flight line were T-28 Trojans and O-1 Birddogs used by the legendary Forward Air Controller (FAC) group, the Ravens.

Then they saw it, a full set of shops: sheet metal, engine, and avionics. The Air Commando Wing's flight school was training Thai and Laotian pilots to fly T-28s. Their job would be to work on the radios in these aircraft.

The shop looked like any other, except the men working there wore fatigues instead of shop clothes. Sergeant Dennis turned out to be more than a supervisor. He was a friend to his men. "He taught me how to play the harmonica properly," Lance explained.

"One day, I mentioned I played the harmonica, and he said, 'Bring it in and let's hear you play.' I brought it with me the next day, and he said, 'You don't know how to play.' He showed me how to play both sides of the instrument and how to play better, like how to play Blues. You learn harmonica by ear. You pull and push to make notes. Sucking or blowing real hard bends the notes to make them flat or sharp. I had played only basic stuff like *Turkey in the Straw* and the old seafarer's song, *Blow the Man Down*."

Lance improved his skill with the instrument, a nice diversion on occasion.

Going Up Country

Despite what he had heard about better pay, working in Thailand did not qualify for the combat rate; that was for those who went to Vietnam. While in Udorn, however, Lance met fellow servicemen returning from "up country." That meant Laos, where the CIA was waging the Secret War against an estimated 35,000 North Vietnamese troops. Those troops, along with the pro-communist Pathet Lao, controlled the Ho Chi Minh Trail, the main supply route that cut through Laos to South Vietnam.

Stories of great adventure and even getting to fly in the back seat of the Birddogs intrigued Lance. He gave it some thought. He too could go "up country," but that was close to the fighting. Then again, in Laos, he would finally get combat pay. He volunteered. Since he was assigned to a secret operation, he could not speak of it for ten years.

Starting in September 1968, he took the daily shuttle, code name: Alley Cat,[26] from Udorn to Vientiane, a city on the Mekong River across the border from Thailand. Vientiane was the administrative capital of Laos.

In a process known as "sheep dipping," every morning Lance and the others turned in their identification and Geneva Convention papers and were given embassy attaché diplomatic cards in return. They were to travel as civilians. There would be no protection if they were captured—and no one had ever escaped.

The secret operation named the "Steve Canyon Program," attracted Thai mercenaries, pirate-type characters who flew the T-28s alongside the famous Ravens in their Birddogs.

Although their cultures and personalities may have differed from one another, they were on the same side, fighting the same enemy. There was much adventure ahead for Lance at this, the height of the Vietnam War.

---

[26] The shuttle, code name Alley Cat, would be a Curtiss C-46 Commando, a deHavilland DHC-4 Caribou, or a C-123K Provider flown by Air America.

His primary job was to repair and replace radio equipment in the airplanes. If no radio work was needed, Lance loaded and armed bombs and rockets and helped pull T-28 props through the starting sequence of their radial engines. He also fueled the airplanes.

"We had to move fifty-five-gallon drums by hand, rolling them on their edges out of the C-130s to where the airplanes were parked. There were no forklifts. We'd take the cap off, put a hand pump on the drum, and pull the handle, first three times this way, then three times that way, and that was one gallon.

"The Birddogs held fifty to fifty-four gallons, which meant we only had to pump one barrel. The T-28s held about two hundred fifty gallons or about five barrels. When an Esso fuel truck was delivered to our base, it was a welcome piece of equipment. It relieved us from all that pumping."

Lance's strength and agility also showed in the way he leaped atop the airplanes. "When the pilots returned from a mission and needed their radios fixed, they'd signal by cupping their hands over their ears. With the propeller spinning only a few feet from me, I'd grasp the fifty-caliber machine gun sticking out from the leading edge of the wing and swing myself up about five feet, landing on top of the wing. That would put me next to the cockpit so the pilot could tell me his radio problem."

Deeper in Laos

Three months after joining the operation, he went further "up country" to work in Muang Soui, Laos, for assignment in Project 404, code name: Palace Dog.

Each morning, Lance and the rest of the crew left the base at Udorn before sunrise. After thirty or forty minutes in a C-46, they'd reach Vientiane, deplane, and wait for the second leg, an hour-long flight to Muang Soui.

The secret air base was labeled "Lima 108" on military maps. Its runway was made of pierced steel planking. The metal mat was laid over the red dirt where nothing grew because of the Agent Orange dropped there regularly. The men spent most of their time on the contaminated flight line. Only a couple of small buildings and bunkers provided shelter from the elements or enemy attack.

On the first day of this new assignment, the men were given flak jackets and helmets before leaving Vientiane to protect them from bullets and grenade shrapnel.

"By the time we reached Muang Soui, we were terrified. Flak jackets? Helmets? Guns? I'd told them before that we weren't soldiers; we were avionics techs! I was trying to hold my M-16 out of the dirt to keep it from jamming while working on airplanes. The gun was heavy, the air was hot, and I was always looking over my shoulder afraid of being shot."

Lance worked all day as airplanes took off on sorties,[27] returned for fuel and ammunition, then left for more sorties. After the first day on the job, the crew shed their helmets and flak jackets.

---

[27] A military attack or reconnaissance mission by an aircraft or other vessel. From the French word meaning *exit*.

"We couldn't deal with it, the heat, the fear you wear when you don those things. Plus, we tried to convince ourselves we were safe, far enough away. We hadn't been attacked yet. I thought, *I could reach my gun if I have to*."

The fighting was closer than Lance realized. T-28 bombing missions rarely lasted over thirty minutes, and the Ravens were only in the air for a couple of hours at a time, hunting down enemy targets and leading bombers to their location.

The Pathet Lao and North Vietnamese controlled most of the low ground at that time. The U.S.-supported Hmong and Royalists controlled the air and had strongholds on the mountaintops; some were only accessible by airstrips carved into the rugged terrain.

The enemy was not the only danger. The cliff at the end of the runway in Muang Soui didn't leave much room for mistakes. A T-28 was on takeoff, then word came it had crashed. Lance jumped on a bomb jammer and rode down the flight line only to find the airplane turned around, upside-down, and the canopy open. He saw fuel spilling out and heard the boost pumps running, sending more fuel into the engine. Charging up with his GI-issue P-38 folding pocket can opener, Lance accessed the battery compartment and disconnected the battery, preventing an explosion, while others removed the pilot from the cockpit.

A Sikorsky "Jolly Green Giant" helicopter landed, and rescuers jumped out and went to work saving the pilot. They placed him in inflatable casts before transporting him to the hospital in Udorn. He survived.

No one knew at the time who called in the helicopter, but many years later at Johnson Space Center, Lance worked alongside retired Air Force Colonel James "Bruce" Broussard, who flew F-105s out of Thailand. The Colonel mentioned having seen a T-28 crash on takeoff in Laos.

"He was the one who called the air ambulance. He was in the 333rd Fighter Group, Takhli Royal Air Base in Thailand. He said the rescuers involved were told they would receive bronze stars, but they never did." Probably, Lance surmised, because these were secret operations.

In Muang Soui, Lance asked to ride along on a mission in a T-28. A commander named Bob agreed to take him. Mounted on the plane were two 50-caliber machine guns plus rockets and bombs and about ten tubes full of cluster bombs. They could fire the bombs one at a time or all at once.

Lance was in the back seat, Bob in the front. They flew into a fortification and saw the shooting below. Bob dove the airplane in, dropped the load of cluster bombs on the target, pulled up, and rolled inverted to watch where they hit.

"*Boom! Boom! Boom! Boom! Boom!* Flashes on the ground! It was a thrill to go inverted because I wasn't used to that, and a thrill to see the cluster bombs go off. I couldn't see any people down there, but anyone down there would have been dead."

Seeing the fighting jolted Lance to reality. He realized after that flight just how close they were.

"Since I'd been working at the airport, I saw some airplanes return damaged. Some didn't come back, but that was all I knew. It didn't sink in until I saw it right in front of me."

The heat and stress were high, and young men found ways to cope with it. At day's end, the crew returned to

Udorn, changed into their fatigues, and once off base changed back into civvies to go out partying all night. Udorn and Laos were a "boys' world." There were plenty of local gals interested in American men.

"Most guys had lots of girlfriends. We went out to bars and listened to good Thai bands, and the girls were everywhere hanging off us."

Lance, however, fell in love with one local Thai woman. He had a house built for her and planned to marry her after the war was over.

Attack at Muang Soui

February 9, 1969. The crew would spend the night in Muang Soui. Lance's supervisor told him he could return to Udorn for the night as usual since they didn't need him for the overnight work. The next day would be a normal workday.

That evening, overnighters set up a wall tent at the airport, a short distance from the commanders' and advisors' house and the command post building. Sodas and C-rations were delivered.

In the early morning hours of February 10, twenty North Vietnamese commandos, called "sappers," shot RPGs and AK-47s into the house and set it on fire. U.S. Special Forces Captain, Joseph Kerr Bush Jr. of Temple, Texas, shot back and tossed grenades, killing two of the enemy force. He drew the sappers away from the house and the tent, but was killed in the heroic fight to save the lives of his fellow Americans and the Laotians with them.

Edgar "Pop" Buell was in the house too. Pop had become a humanitarian aid worker after his wife passed away. He was a Hoosier farmer who had volunteered to come to Laos as an agricultural advisor. Pop threw a mattress over himself when the enemy sprayed the house with bullets. None hit him.

Lance's co-workers in the tent may have been spared because it hadn't yet been set up when the sappers staked the place out during the daylight, and they didn't see it in the dark of night. They aimed their rocket grenades at the house and the command post.

The next morning, Lance and a medic, Charles Buckley, returned. They removed Captain Bush's body from the burned house. Lance picked up some RPG tails and saw pieces of scalp on the ground. He heard enemy bodies were hanging from the fence being burned with gasoline, but he didn't want to see that.

One of the hardest things Lance saw that day was twenty bodies of Laotian soldiers and maybe some Thai among them.

"They were there to defend us. Their bodies were taken to another building, wrapped in gauze, and their hats placed on their heads. Smoking was pretty common then. Cigarettes were how we traded things. It hurts me still. I saw a cigarette placed between the fingers of a dead Laotian soldier. His comrades kept the cigarette lit until he was finally laid to rest. I'm still emotional about it now. I think about it a couple of times a week."

Trying to keep the war a secret, the Nixon Administration announced that Captain Bush was killed in a "non-combat action." The facts could not stay suppressed forever, and Captain Bush was posthumously awarded the Bronze Star and the Silver Star Medal of Valor. However, the secret, now a lie, is maintained today by the denial of veterans' benefits to some who served in this place.

On to Shangri-La

Lance continued to work in Muang Soui after the attack. He stayed there until a job opened in Luang Prabang. He would be put in charge of the bomb depot storing bombs that arrived in Air America C-130s.

On arrival in Luang Prabang, a CIA agent approached him, handing him a Colt .38 Special, a five-shot revolver, and said, "This is for you."

Lance nodded and took the gun.

"No, this is for you." The agent was emphatic.

"Okay." Lance thought he understood, but the agent knew he didn't, yet.

"No, this is for *you*. For you to shoot yourself if the Pathet Lao comes." Nobody wanted to be captured by the Pathet Lao.

Even though everyone had warned that Luang Prabang was a scary place, it was also a seductively beautiful city. "Luang Prabang was the closest thing to Shangri-La I can think of. It's a gorgeous little town in the mountains near China. There's a mountain in the middle of the city, and the Mekong and Nam Khan Rivers come together there. They have beautiful temples called Wats, and the royal palace where the king lived. I understood the Pathet Lao still respected or revered the king, and the city of Luang Prabang was off limits."

That was mostly true while Lance was in this beautiful place. But before he arrived, the Pathet Lao had twice attacked the airport, code name: Lima 54, and the air attaché house. Despite this, Lance considered it "a good duty—way better than anywhere else I'd been in Laos."

All the guys shared a two-story house. Lance and a roommate had an upstairs bedroom. House girls and boys cleaned, and chefs cooked for them. They called the commander Mr. Moody instead of Commander since they were there in secret. Everyone else was on a first-name basis regardless of rank.

Lance reflected on more of the things he liked about being stationed in Luang Prabang. "We had a projector and watched movies. A C-130 brought supplies, armament, bombs, and ammo a couple of times a week. We lived well and had good food considering this was the military. Some of the guys have been back and say the house is still there."

There was, however, trouble in Shangri-La. In case of attack, Lance and his roommate kept grenades under their beds and on top of the wardrobes that separated them. In constant fear of the enemy nearby, he stuck masking tape around the grenades' spoons, pulled out the pins, and slept with live grenades under his pillow. The extra few seconds this would give him could make the difference in survival. Next to his bed were an M-16, M-14, an M-1 Garand, and a Thompson submachine gun, all loaded.

They stayed in communication with personnel in Vientiane and Udorn for reports on the enemy's movement. One night, an Intelligence officer reported the Pathet Lao was three kilometers away. The men were on high alert.

"I thought we would be killed when Ed Boggs came in our room asking if I could hear them. He said he could hear them coming. I didn't hear what Ed heard, and he returned to his room for a while. He came back after a bit and said he figured out what it was. He slept with a pillow over his head and was hearing his heartbeat."

Living in these conditions can wreak havoc on the mind, not knowing what will happen next. Ed Gunter was one of those FACs, the guys who flew the Birddogs to find where the enemy was hiding. At the dinner table one night, Ed told everyone the Pathet Lao was really close.

"He told us to remain alert all night. A couple of nurses were visiting for dinner. Suddenly, there was a big explosion. The window broke. I panicked. I was terrified. But Ed and Mr. Mooney seemed amused. They laughed at us, then admitted they had one of the cooks tape an M-80 firecracker to the window and light it."

Lance felt totally unprepared in the moment, inadequate to the situation. "I thought, *where do I go? What do I do? Where should I hide? Where are my weapons?* My weapons were upstairs. There was no place to hide. We had no foxholes, shelters, or bunkers like we did in Muang Soui; we just had a house. I was mad at myself for panicking and being confused. Those nurses were white as a sheet, and I probably was too."

The men faced dangers everywhere. The facilities where they worked were always susceptible to attack. Despite the tension, the beauty of Luang Prabang captured Lance's heart. It is the one place he would like to return to in Laos.

He had extended his tour by six months and asked if he could stay longer. They regarded what they were doing as a good thing and had reason to be there. "Being immersed in it, all of us believed in what we were doing, helping the Laotians save their country. We knew all the Laotians we worked with were good people. We loved them, and they loved us. That motivated me. I wanted to stay and do what I could to help them."

Most of the previous commanders didn't have a problem with guys staying because they had experience. But their unit's new commander said, "No, you boys have a tendency to go native and we don't want that. You need to go back home and be an American."

In April 1970, after twenty months in Southeast Asia, Lance caught the Alley Cat shuttle to Udorn for the last time. If he could survive the journey, he would change planes in Saigon, and fly home to the United States. While he didn't want to leave, he was in a dangerous place. "Boarding the plane in Saigon felt surreal. I thought we would be shot down and I was very afraid."

They weren't shot down and Lance was given safe passage out of Southeast Asia. Back on home soil, he was honorably discharged.

A New Life

Like so many veterans of foreign wars, Lance didn't know what to do when he returned. He picked Houston as his new home because his brother was living there. There was also plenty of work for a guy with Lance's skills. He became a partner in Associated Radio Service Company at Hobby Airport.

Houston was a good place for Lance. He met Christine, a tall, lovely redhead with a knockout smile. She lived several houses down from Lance's brother and worked in the neighborhood Stop N Go. Lance would come in to buy cigarettes and was smitten, but too shy to ask her out. His sister-in-law, who was Christine's friend, convinced him to ask her on a date.

"I felt awkward at first, but I took her out on my motorcycle, and later I rented a Cessna 150 and took her flying. She loved it."

They married in October 1972. By then, Lance managed the AirTronics avionics shop, which included servicing NASA's T-38s and B-57s at Ellington Air Force Base. Their first son was just born when a contractor he worked with mentioned a job with Bell Helicopter. The opportunity was in Iran. Working overseas interested Lance—he liked to travel, see the world, and make more money, tax-free. When Bell called for an interview, Lance got his first haircut since leaving the Air Force.

He moved his little family to Isphahani, Iran, in November 1973, and within three years their family grew again, welcoming their second son.

With his electronics experience from the Vietnam War, plus what Bell had given him, Lance rose from Shop Supervisor to Armament Engineer. The family moved to Tehran, and by age thirty-two he had become the Chief Armament Engineer on all U.S. military helicopters in Iran.

"We didn't realize the Iranian revolution was taking place until it was well on its way. The conflicts were happening on the south end, but we were in the middle and north end. We watched censored English-language TV, so there was no word of insurrection and violence. I learned of the revolution through ham radio."

By August 1978, getting their oldest son to school had become difficult due to the chaos. Stores closed at night. Gasoline was hard to find. The situation was too dangerous for the family, so Lance accompanied Christine and the boys home to Texas, and then he went back.

"The revolution was bad. At night, I heard a lot of gunfire and people chanting in the streets. Those were frightening times. Power would go off at eight o'clock every night. There was a curfew, and you'd be shot if seen outside. Herds of people would come down the street, shouting."

Lance found "Yankee go home" spray-painted on the front gate to his house, so he sold his furniture and car for ten cents on the dollar and moved in with friend and co-worker, Ken Ramey. If it got better, they thought, they'd bring their families back.

However, conditions didn't improve. Lance and Ken lay on the bare apartment floor at night, listening by shortwave to the BBC to find out what was happening on Eisenhower Street.

"We stayed up all night, played a moonshot game, and recorded crowds of people chanting. Then one night, we heard them coming up the street. It was winter. We stuffed our jackets full of candy bars. I had a BB gun with one shot, a knife, and a flashlight."

Their escape plan was to get on the roof and run from house to house, which they could do because all the houses were connected.

"I thought that was the end when I heard them come up the street. The airport had been closed, so we couldn't get out."

Fortunately, they didn't have to put the escape plan into action that night. Just in time, they heard the airport would be opened briefly in the morning. Lance and Ken already had open-date return tickets on KLM and an American Express card, so they went to the Bell office, resigned, and took a taxi to the airport.

"On the way out, it was a cliffhanger. People mobbed the airport. We didn't see any other Americans. Security officials took our passports, passed them around for others to look at, and finally stamped them. They frisked us and checked through our luggage. I thought at any time we'd be stopped."

The pair watched carefully as they climbed the air stairs. Most passengers on board were Iranians. Intense silence filled the cabin. Even as the engines started, Lance was anxious.

"We started to taxi, and I was thinking they're going to come get us."

When the airplane lifted off the runway, and the main gear came up, cheers replaced the oppressive silence, and they flew on to Amsterdam.

Time and Space

Back in Houston, Lance joined Boeing's electronics team at Johnson Space Center in the Shuttle Avionics Integration Laboratory. He worked nights, attended school during the day, and earned an Associate Degree in Aviation Maintenance Technology.

When a navigation aid engineer position opened with Rockwell, Lance applied with confidence. Even though he wasn't a degreed engineer, he knew more about navaids than most. Rockwell hired him as one of two Shuttle navaids engineers in Orbiter Engineering. He took home volumes of books to study because the Shuttle wasn't something one could learn in college. He had to know everything about its electronics, all the wires, and the data.

"It's very complex. I was sleeping and dreaming in machine language. The electronics on the Shuttle were intelligent, like an insect. Maybe not as smart as a bird, but smart, and had situational awareness. The artificial autonomic nervous system knew if it was hot or cold, was over here or there, kind of like a living thing. That was even from the beginning of the Shuttle.

"The astronauts demanded they be able to fly and land it, but the Shuttle always could have done all that by itself. They only took over the landing once they crossed over the heading alignment cone that guided the Shuttle onto the runway centerline. Up to that point, the flying was automated."

Boeing bought Rockwell Aerospace in 1996 and in 2002, Lance was made the Space Shuttle Navaids Subsystem Manager. In any situation regarding navigational aids, the buck stopped with him. He held this position until retirement in 2008, after twenty-nine years at the Space Center. As a consultant for Boeing, when the last Space Shuttle mission flew in 2011, Lance was one of a small cadre of folks who had worked every single mission.

After retirement, he wanted a simple life, but the pace has not been slow. Thanks to his grandfather, Dewey Bonbrake, and the wonderfully mysterious Philmont radio, Lance took what his dad and grandfather taught him and opened Borden Radio Company. He sells kits worldwide for building crystal radios like the ones used by GIs in foxholes in World War II, and like the one that brought magic to Lance and his brother Jim in Atlanta in 1953.

Hanoi Taxi

Mike: I learned about the massive Lockheed C-141 Starlifter that was tucked in the corner of the ramp in Reno, Nevada, from Jan, the customer service representative at Mercury Air Center. "It's some sort of flying museum," she told me. "They used it to fly troops home from Vietnam."

The plane brought back memories. My dad's office was in San Bernardino, California, near Norton Air Force Base. Several C-141s were parked there between trips to Southeast Asia, their tails almost overhanging the fence along East 3rd Street.

The Starlifter was the hulking workhorse of the U.S. Air Force's heavy lift fleet. Every time I took off from Blythe carrying canceled checks in a Piper Lance, I watched for the lumbering transports to cross in front of me. They swept along a ridge, maybe 500 feet above it, in low-level training over the barren desert.

But here was a special Starlifter, registration number 66-0177, the Hanoi Taxi. It was one of fifteen C-141s in the operation that carried our prisoners of war home from Hanoi. This particular day in Reno, I only had a few minutes to observe people filtering through its front doors and eventually down the ramp out the airplane's rear. Near the exit, shielded by

Plexiglas, was a panel covered with signatures of the POWs it carried and the dates of their interment.

Decades have passed since Operation Homecoming. On that first day, the Hanoi Taxi and two other C-141s flew one hundred and sixteen POWs to Clark Air Base in the Philippines, then to Norton for emotionally wrenching reunions with loved ones.

Fifty-four flights brought home 591 of our boys between February 12 and April 4, 1973. Among them was USAF Colonel George Everett "Bud" Day, who spent over five years and seven months in the hellhole prison dubbed the Hanoi Hilton. He was one of the last soldiers from the Vietnam War to receive the Medal of Honor. Senator John McCain was imprisoned for five-and-a-half years. Congressman Samuel Robert Johnson of Texas' 3rd Congressional District spent nearly seven years in the prison. Of those years, nearly three and a half were in solitary confinement, shackled to a slab of concrete. His captors continually tortured him and the other prisoners.

Another prisoner, naval aviator Jeremiah Andrew Denton Jr., later a Rear Admiral and a U.S. Senator from Alabama, was forced to participate in a televised North Vietnamese propaganda interview in 1966. During the interview, he kept blinking his eyes. Viewers and commentators thought there was something wrong with him. There was, but it wasn't a nervous twitch. He was using Morse code to spell out T-O-R-T-U-R-E. When he stepped off the airplane at Clark Air Base, he had been a POW for nearly eight years.

Each prisoner suffered defending our freedom along with more than 58,000 soldiers who paid the ultimate sacrifice—

many of them still missing in action, their bodies never recovered. About eighty percent of the missing are airmen shot down over Vietnam and Laos.

This airplane represented the story of those it brought home, as well as those it didn't. Inside, the scene would have been like that in the first of these Starlifters. As its wheels left the runway in Hanoi, the pilots heard commotion from the rear of the airplane. Cheers eclipsed the thunder of four turbojet engines at takeoff power. The homecoming celebration had begun.

When the Hanoi Taxi was not on display as a museum, it served as a transport aircraft and flew relief missions. In 2006, forty years after its maiden flight, 66-0177 was retired to The Museum of the US Air Force in Dayton, Ohio, where visitors can appreciate it today. If you listen carefully, you can hear the echoes—shouts, hoots, and hollers from POWs heading home from North Vietnam.

Plages Sombres

Mike: I stand in quiet survey of the scene, cold water crashing on the shore before me. A faint murmur accents the air, emerging quickly into a crackling roar. In seconds, a French Mirage fighter jet dressed in camouflage screams past me, a hundred feet above the churning English Channel. The pilot banks hard north in salute to those below, then disappears in the distance. Silence returns.

Turning from the overlook, a lush green carpet of grass spotted by immaculately maintained trees unfolds behind me. There, in perfect symmetry, ten thousand white marble crosses declare the war is over. Winter may be the time to visit this place as there are no crowds to compete with contemplation. Nothing, except for an occasional military jet flying by to pay respects to the soldiers buried here.

I learned of the D-Day invasion in school, history books, and movies, but standing here in the Normandy American Military Cemetery and Memorial, the realization sinks much deeper. Touching the sand of Omaha Beach, one cannot fathom the terror and dedication those who took part in this colossal undertaking must have felt. I step with humble reverence around the headstones, reading names—many *Known but to God*. Over fifteen hundred names of sons who were never recovered or identified are etched in a circular stone wall. If they could, they'd speak of family, of going home.

During my flying career, I have been afforded some grand opportunities. For the first two weeks of December 2013, my job required a return to Paris. I wasn't interested in spending my free time there, so one weekend I rented a car, took on the challenge of French traffic circles, and got the heck out of Dodge.

On June 6, 1944, these brave souls and others spilled their blood so that we might remain free. The price paid during the D-Day campaign was fifty thousand Allied lives, another one hundred fifty thousand wounded.

As I drive around Normandy, I can't imagine war ever touching this landscape of low, rolling terrain graced with long rock walls and hedgerows, quaint farms, cottages, and stone chapels. Yet, here is the evidence, a rusting cannon sitting on its side at a field's edge, ruins of buildings left for the memory. Museums and historical markers populate the villages.

At Pointe Du Hoc lies a moonscape of massive craters from bombs dropped to secure the planned offensive, shattering fortifications that once overlooked both Omaha and Utah beaches. Here, the cold winter wind seems to cut into me as the rain falls, while I enter preserved bunkers, thinking hard about the fate of those once inside.

Look, out on the beaches, where U.S. Army Rangers climbed these hundred-foot cliffs, taking this ground in the early morning hours of the invasion. Their losses were heavy as they stood off several counterattacks until relief came the next day.

Near the memorial, two flagpoles champion United States flags hung at half-staff. At sunset, life in the cemetery pauses, the flags are lowered, and all who are breathing salute or place their hand over their heart, while *Taps* is played. I behold what is about me, and I whisper, "Thank you."

Two

Guest Contributor, Ryszard Zadow

A good wingman says nothing but "Two" and "You're on fire."[28]

Yesterday I got to spend some time flying as the number two position in a formation of old warbirds. I was flying a T-6 Texan, and hangin' onto the wingtip of the lead aircraft, a T-28. For me, it was a place that was...perfect.

My second airplane ride was in a T-6 named Thunder Chicken. I was fifteen years old. The T-6 was parked in the grass at Weiser Airport in Cypress, Texas. We didn't know it was Cypress, Texas, back then; it was just an airport in the middle of nowhere. I took my first flying lesson there in a Civil Air Patrol Cessna 150. I was in awe of the T-6. Its owners, Al Snyder and Pete Howard, were ten feet tall to me. One day, Al Snyder was tinkering with Thunder Chicken. I sheepishly walked up and asked him if I could climb up and look inside. He said, "Ok...just don't touch nuthin'."

---

[28] Fighter jets go out in pairs: a lead and a wingman. The wingman must have 100% loyalty. The wingman's response to a command given by the lead plane is either their tactical call sign, or just "Two," because he is in position number two.

It felt like climbing onto a skyscraper. I must've stood outside the front cockpit for ten minutes, trying to absorb every detail. Wonder is the only emotion I felt. I finally climbed down and thanked Al. I got about fifteen steps away when I heard him say, "Hey, kid!" I spun around, and he said, "You want to go for a ride?" I blurted out, "Yes, sir!"

Al strapped me in, and for the next forty-five minutes or so, the only emotion I felt was awe. I was totally captivated by the sights, sounds, smells, and feel of that grumbly old airplane. Once airborne, he told me to try it. I flew around in a gentle 360-degree turn; then he said, "Here, let's try this…"

Then the airplane started a nose dive; a pull-up, and there were forces pushing me into my seat I'd never felt before. In no time, the world was upside down, and it was much quieter. Then I'm looking over his head at nothing but the earth, and those forces pushed me into my seat again. The old airplane groaned and rattled. Awe shifted to ecstasy! I'd confirmed this was my calling and could hardly contain myself.

I had to get home before my parents returned. I'd taken the car and didn't have a driver's license. I kept thanking Mr. Snyder as I hurried away, explaining to him why I was in a rush, and he just laughed. It was a defining moment.

So yesterday, I'm hanging on the wingtip of a T-28. It's a sacred place for me. We all have our way of dealing with the world when it comes crashing in. For me, I drift back to the days when I was just a lieutenant in a fighter squadron. When life was simple. When you earned your keep by how well you flew; how good a wingman you were; how well you could lead your buddies into combat; and how well you landed on the boat.

Life was measured in success and failures that simply let you live another day, and you didn't know any better to stress over it. Many days have passed since then, but that doesn't mean I can't go back there in my mind. When you're hangin' onto the wingtip of a T-28, there are no problems in your life.

To the uninitiated, it would appear you have to concentrate and focus all your thoughts on being a few mere feet from another airplane in flight, but truth be known, for those who once did that as a matter of course, it's a relaxing place, a place to ponder. It's a place to let your mind and heart bask in the wonderment of what God created. The sky, the land, the smoothness of the air. The noise, the smell, the vibration of the machine God gave man the skills to create. The Awe. The same I felt standing on the wing of Thunder Chicken. The humility of being human.

My manipulation of the flight controls is subconscious as I hold my position, mimicking the movement of the lead plane. I think of my brother-in-law who just passed away. The day also marks one year ago that I lost another person close to me. It's not always death that takes people from our lives, but often decisions. When someone you love passes on, it's so final. When you lose a relationship to life's different paths, it's loss just the same.

So for that short time yesterday that I flew an old T-6, a peer to Thunder Chicken, I got to meditate in that sacred place, a few mere feet from the wingtip of a T-28. It was for me, perfect. And in my backseat, his first flight in a grumbly old T-6 was a fifteen-year-old kid.

Ryszard Zadow is a Texan, a Southwest Airlines captain, and former LCDR, US Navy.

The Courageous

The sea is dangerous and its storms terrible, but these obstacles have never been sufficient reason to remain ashore… Unlike the mediocre, intrepid spirits seek victory over those things that seem impossible… It is with an iron will that they embark on the most daring of all endeavors… to meet the shadowy future … and conquer the unknown.

—Ferdinand Magellan, c. 1520

The Real Rosie the Riveter

Mike: Vickie's mom grew up on a farm as one of nine children. Farm kids know you do what it takes to make things work, and sometimes you fix them with what's on hand. When she married, she learned how to build houses. That skill was more valuable when she became a widow and had to leave Kentucky with her two young children in search of work.

In the Willow Run neighborhood of Ypsilanti, Michigan, Henry Ford had made his factory available for building B-24s. When Vickie's mom heard there was work in Michigan, she and her children boarded a bus that headed north.

Times were tough during World War II, and a job in the bomber factory was a good deal. Manufacturers turned out one plane every fifty-five minutes, thanks to the handiwork of America's women. Collectively, they were called "Rosie the Riveter," after a popular song of the day. But there was not just one Rosie; there were six million who went into the factories to replace the men who had gone to war.

When actor Walter Pidgeon visited the Willow Run assembly line to film a promotion for war bonds, the crew looked for the woman who would be the human face of that spirit, the woman who embodied courage, strength, and determination.

Someone at the plant declared they had the perfect candidate right there, building airplanes. She was spunky and gutsy, fit the character of the song, her primary job was riveting, and her name really was Rose.

Linda: That all happened before Vickie was born, but she loves telling the story about her mom, Rose Will Monroe, the original Rosie the Riveter.

The familiar poster of the lady sporting a red bandana and flexing her bicep was not the original. That was a Westinghouse company morale poster created later. The emblem on the model's collar is a Westinghouse badge. That model was Geraldine Hoff Doyle, a musician. But after a couple of weeks working in the factory, she decided the risk to her hands was too great. Not willing to sacrifice her future in music, she quit the job. But she was there the day the photographer took pictures. Years later, that Westinghouse company poster became the symbol of Rosie the Riveter. Geraldine wasn't even aware they had used her likeness until decades later.

Rose had long admired the women who came to pick up the airplanes she helped build. Watching the Women Airforce Service Pilots fly away relying on her rivets, she longed to be one of them. The rules forbade her, a widow with children, to join the WASP. Despite her circumstances, her heart belonged in those airplanes.

In the early 1970s, Rose finally became a pilot. She shared her love of flight infectiously for a few years until one day when a passenger changed the course of her life. In his first flight in a small plane, the passenger reached forward on takeoff and flipped the switch that operated the electric flaps asking, "What's this do?"

What it did was slam the plane into the ground, causing serious injuries to Rose, her passenger, and Vickie, who was in the back seat. Rose lost an eye and a kidney, and she never fully recovered her health.

Says Vickie, "It seems so final, but it's not. Mom left a legacy for all. She was uncompromising in her high standards, no job was beneath her, and she believed teamwork could accomplish anything."

For certain, she was the spirit of "We Can Do It." The woman who became the human face of Rosie the Riveter while building B-24s worked hard, had a zest for life, and never knew failure—not because she never failed, but because she never gave up. But don your parachute, we're about to take a leap. Her daughter inherited that spunk.

Mike: Although she enjoyed learning about flying from her mom, Vickie was eager to live her life her way when she was out of school. After some time in New Mexico that included a horse, a dog, a marriage, and a child, Vickie became a single mom and moved to Indiana for a restart. She opened a water treatment business and considered earning her pilot certificate to more efficiently reach customers.

But flying took a back seat or, should I say, Vickie took one, when someone introduced her to skydiving. The world of flying returned anew. Instead of being up front at the controls, following in her mother's wake, Rose's youngest child moved to where there was easy access to the door for jumping *out*.

While working at the Clark County Airport in southern Indiana, Vickie became a professional skydiver. She joined the Aerial Allstars Skydiving Team and was one of the few people performing a unique night pyrotechnic routine. Control boxes strapped to her arms were wired underneath her jumpsuit, connected to pyro tubes attached to her feet. During a jump, she'd monitor the altimeter on her wrist, pressing switches to release fireworks at predetermined altitudes, leaving the crowds in awe.

One of her biggest fans, Rose loved watching her daughter's shows, saying if her health were better, she would jump with them. She often rode in the airplane with the troupe, enjoying a bird's-eye view of the streaming sparklers. The inspiration was mutual, and Vickie renewed her flying lessons. With a scholarship from the Ninety-Nines, she grew to know and appreciate her mother's passion and finally earned her pilot certificate.

Linda: A bus ride while visiting Cancun offered more fireworks. Wyn Croston, a dashing U.S. Air Force captain, electrical engineer, and missile launch officer, took the last open seat on the bus. Exchanging phone numbers led to a whirlwind romance and Wyn's introduction to skydiving. "I fell for her," he chuckled, while explaining their first kiss was during a freefall jump.

Wyn and Vickie Croston have used their airplane to fly people and pets in need, as volunteers with Angel Flight, Young Eagles, Challenge Air, and Pilots N Paws.

Vickie reflects proudly, yet humbly, on her mother's accomplishments and influence. "Mom was inducted posthumously into the Kentucky Aviation Hall of Fame for her role supporting the war effort as Rosie the Riveter."

The Rose Monroe Society raised funds to support the National World War II Memorial. At the groundbreaking ceremony, Vickie was joined by Colin Powell, Tom Hanks, Elizabeth Dole, and others. Then a woman introduced herself as Mrs. Smith and asked Vickie, "What's your connection with the Memorial?"

When Vickie told of her famous mother, Mrs. Smith insisted that Vickie stay put while she fetched her son. Moments later, FedEx founder Fred Smith was ushered over to shake Vickie's hand, and they discussed the importance of the National Memorial and of leaving a legacy, as that Kentucky farm girl did.

A Picture of Courage

** Contains some graphic description of war*

Linda: I met Chris Sullivan as a fellow cross-country air racer in 2016. It was his first race, and he was admittedly nervous.

"I'd always wanted to learn to fly. When I discovered Able Flight, I submitted my application for a scholarship and was selected to come to Purdue University for training."

Chris' first flight was in May 2014 in a Sky Arrow, an aircraft equipped with adaptive rudder controls, when he entered Able Flight's intensive training course nine years after being hit by sniper fire.

It was May 21, 2005. The 256th Infantry Brigade, Louisiana Army National Guard, had been tasked with locating and disarming IEDs just outside Baghdad Airport. As the team worked carefully, the enemy watched. Suddenly, bullets flew, one entering Chris' neck and exiting his back.

Nobody else was hit. Sergeant Sullivan lay on the ground, bleeding from his neck. He couldn't move or speak. His vocal cords burned but he felt no pain; the sniper's bullet had severed his spine. His squad frantically laid down suppression fire and attempted to evacuate him. They were doing their job, just as they had been trained.

Carried to safety behind a Humvee, Chris could hear the radio. Apache helicopters were needed to blanket the area with more suppression fire for Blackhawk helicopters to swoop in for the rescue, but the Apaches were on other missions. He knew they were too far to reach him before he bled to death, but he wasn't afraid.

He prayed, "Lord, if it's time to bring me home, I'm okay with that, but I will fight it as long as I can because I have so much more to do." Unable to speak well, he smiled, hoping it would calm his buddies as his blood spilled out.

Then, over the radio squelched the news: two Apaches were within three miles and on their way, *hot and heavy*—fully loaded with ammo!

God didn't bring Chris home to heaven that day, and so began the long, painful road to recovery. Knowing his company would return from deployment in three-and-a-half months, he wanted to greet them, so he asked the doctors for an aggressive rehab plan. That reunion stateside was a great motivator, but once back home in Mire, Louisiana, doubt and fear prowled around him as he fought against post-traumatic stress. What was his purpose, now that he was paralyzed?

Chris found his purpose in helping veterans through the Veterans Administration, with empathy that only someone who has been there can have. Four years later, he joined Louisiana State Representative Rodney Alexander's staff as a caseworker for wounded warriors.

He shared his story at fundraisers and despite his paralysis, he learned to scuba dive, went skydiving, and became a

National Veterans Wheelchair Games silver medalist in snow skiing. And on the second anniversary of being wounded, our hero began dating his future wife, later witnessing another miracle – the birth of their son.

Chris worked hard at Able Flight, in ground school several hours a day and flying twice daily. Then, the night before his check ride, he fell ill with an infection that spread to his bones. Courageously, he fought back for a month and after a full recovery, he returned to Purdue to earn his wings.

Only two years after his first flight, he climbed out of his wheelchair and into the cockpit. The day was hot, so friends helped drape ice-cold cloths on his neck because his body couldn't regulate temperature.

Engines started, props turned, and airplanes taxied to the runway. There in the Sky Arrow, eleven years after facing death in war, Chris Sullivan taxied in line and looked down the row of race planes. A tear came as he took the starting line, throttled up, and became: *a race pilot.* The trophy awarded to him symbolizes so much more than finishing first in his class in that race. It is the fight he wins every day and, "as long as I can, because I have so much more to do."

AnnElise Bennett and The Man Trophy

Since its inception in 2007, all season point winners in the Sport Air Racing League had been men. AnnElise Bennett set out to change that. Awards for the most accumulated points in each category are given at the last race of the year. There are three categories: experimental (amateur-built), production (factory-built), and warbird. Within these categories are classes based on engine size and horsepower, single or twin engine, and whether the airplane has retractable landing gear.

In 2009, her rookie year, AnnElise won second place in her class of factory-built airplanes but finished thirteenth in total points out of over one hundred racers in all categories. When she saw the season awards for first, second, and third in each category, she called them "man trophies" and vowed to claim one the next year. "That giant wood trophy made the angels sing in my head, 'Ooohhh, girl, you gotta get one of those!'"

There are no monetary prizes in SARL. Racers compete for those trophies and bragging rights. For AnnElise, that trophy, those bragging rights were priceless in the male-dominated world of aviation. The only way she would have a chance at the top spot would be to race as many races in the season as possible, collecting points.

Over the next few weeks, she worked on the man trophy plan in her head. She and her husband, Bobby, were both racing—she in her Cessna 182, *X-ray*, and he in his Beechcraft Bonanza. They couldn't afford to go to every race in two airplanes, so she proposed priorities for the 2010 season. Each would fly their own plane to races within Texas, but *X-ray* would take precedence for the distant contests. The next year would be Bobby's turn.

It was crucial to her goal to do it by herself, in her airplane, "so that I was solely responsible for winning or losing that big, beautiful piece of wood"—and the aforementioned priceless bragging rights.

But then the news came. AnnElise's mother had been diagnosed with ovarian cancer, and early in 2010 her health took a turn for the worse. Her mom wasn't afraid of dying, but she feared how her death would affect her family and friends. She wanted them to live life to the fullest, and AnnElise knew that meant grabbing every experience and adventure she could, to show her mother she would be okay.

"Mom was in the hospital several times. My sister and I took turns spending twenty-four-hour shifts with her. And while she wasn't an 'airplane person,' she appreciated that I was and despite declining health, she encouraged me not to miss a single race."

Encouraged by her mother, the year started according to the man trophy plan, with meets in Taylor, Sherman, and Plainview, Texas; and Cecil County, Maryland. The next one, in Mesquite, would be the fourth time she and *X-ray* would face off against Louise "Squeege" Scudieri and her airplane, *Four-One-Mike*. They were both new to SARL the previous year, and that was the first time she had raced anyone with the same airplane.

AnnElise thought back: "I figured she had to want it as badly as I did, being a girl competitor in the boys' club. My highly competitive nature took hold, and I went screaming around the course, flying the straightest, tightest line I could. My speed of 158.10 miles per hour beat Louise's 157.18. I was hooked." Louise was too.

Louise is a Certified Registered Nurse Anesthetist, and CEO and owner of Smooth Inductions, P.C., an independent anesthesia provider. She puts people to sleep and wakes them up nice. As she steps from the operating room to her airplane, she says it is difficult to decide which she loves more. However, when it comes to stress relief, the scales tip in favor of flying and racing.

AnnElise had such a great time planning and racing and felt so good after crossing the finish line that she laughed all the way to the ramp. "I savor the feeling and completely enjoy the experience each time, even when I miss a turn and beat myself up."

SARL races start in speed order, fastest first. Because AnnElise's speed had been 0.75 miles an hour faster than Louise's in Plainview, AnnElise took off first.

Neck-and-neck around the course, as AnnElise called a turn, Louise called the same turn moments later. Inside the cockpits of two 182s, two women sweated, because opening vents and windows would increase aerodynamic drag. In *X-ray*, as in *Four-One-Mike*, the racers' eyes scanned repeatedly from outside to the instrument panel inside.

The time between their radio calls grew shorter with every turn. Each lady kept her right hand on the throttle, her left on the yoke, with intense mental focus to maintain the maximum speed, the straightest line, and the most level flight possible. Louise was closing the gap. When they crossed the finish line, she had crept up on AnnElise, only seconds behind her. That's all it takes.

Louise flew fast, and AnnElise congratulated her on a tight race. Afterward, confusion about the course length and times recorded brought adjustments to the final standings, placing AnnElise first. Given her quest for the man trophy, she needed those points, but she had heard Louise's radio calls and knew her rival was the winner. Being a true competitor, AnnElise declined the first-place points. If the national championship was to be hers, it would be hers fair and square.

Louise's fastest time that year was in that race in Mesquite, Texas, where she clocked 157.31 miles per hour. AnnElise's quickest was in Courtland, Alabama, where she turned in a speed of 164.45. At each event, it seemed everyone held their breath waiting to hear the times and speeds of these two so closely matched.

In addition to the excitement with Louise was the wider picture: with more pilot participation, the season point race had intensified. The roster of top contenders became more crowded with each race. By midsummer, only five races were left. AnnElise could not miss any if she were to earn the coveted prize. But her mother's days were winding down.

"I spent almost every day with Mom in May, June, and July, leaving only to go race with her blessing. She was eager to hear how each race went, and even as her words became fewer, she reminded me I needed to 'go get that big trophy.'"

Her mother passed away two weeks before the Great Canadian Air Rally in August. Flying her 182 to Canada with a side trip to Niagara Falls was what AnnElise called "the Good Fly" and the change of scenery her heart needed.

Races in Pagosa Springs, Colorado; Sherman, Texas; and Courtland, Alabama, all went according to the plan. Her points were piling up. Going into the final race of the year in Taylor, Texas, fifty points were all that separated at least half a dozen racers vying for the three production category awards. Depending on how many airplanes showed up in each class and how the top racers performed, it would be a nail-biter until the last airplane landed.

Louise couldn't make the last race, but a new guy in a 182 arrived at Taylor, a potential threat to AnnElise's year-long strategy. This would be the final obstacle between her and a man trophy.

"I believe that was the most nervous I'd ever been before a race." For every airplane she beat in her class, she would get ten bonus points added to points for placing first, second, or third. On the flip side, any airplane that beat her would get those bonus points. All the other trophy contenders were men. To be the first female SARL champion, she needed every point she could get.

Jason Rovey and his RV-8 had seven airplanes in his class. If he won this last race, he would earn sixty bonus points. There were three in AnnElise's class. Granted, they were in two different categories eligible for a trophy. His airplane was in the experimental category—he built it himself—and hers was factory-built. Still, her personal quest was to be among the top three overall winners.

In her class, a fast Cirrus racer came in first, no surprise. But as new racers are prone to do, the fellow in the 182 took a more leisurely pace around the course. When the results were posted, AnnElise was awarded ninety points for second place. Finishing ahead of the new guy, she garnered another ten bonus points.

She had survived one of the hardest years of her life and competed in ten air races, winning one against Louise and losing one to her. AnnElise finished the season twenty points ahead of Jason, good enough for those bragging rights. She had won the 2010 Sport Air Racing League Bronze National Championship.

"Yes, I got silly with my man trophy and carried it everywhere—to the party, seat-belted in the back of *X-ray* for the ride home, and even to bed with me."

When the race season was over, there was time for reflection. "When my personal results were tallied, I had lost my mom too early, but what I gained were great flying experiences, wonderful new friends, and self-confidence. Setting a huge goal and ultimately accomplishing it in the midst of family tragedy proved I was making the most of every opportunity, living life to the fullest, and I was okay. That's what my mom wanted. I think she would be very proud."

AnnElise Bennett in her not-uncommon pose,
with her beloved X-ray
Photo by Cliff Reese

Sunshine and Handstands

Only two years after saying good-bye to her mother, AnnElise Bennett was handed another family tragedy. A car accident took her precious daughter, Sarah, her "Sunshine Girl," two months before her graduation from Stephen F. Austin State University in Nacogdoches, Texas. AnnElise took charge of her emotional health to feel her way through the darkness of grief. Each of us travels that journey in our own way, and this pilot, air racer, skydiver-dropping lady faces the loss of her twenty-one-year-old child as a pilot-in-command.

AnnElise directs her energy to lifting others up, giving tirelessly with compassion and encouragement. Her heartbreaking circumstances have taught her to meet challenges daily with perspective: to find collateral beauty and to water the flowers, not the weeds.

She created an endowment at the university in Sarah's name, honoring her passion for photography with scholarships. Having long been a fitness buff, AnnElise challenged herself physically with yoga, CrossFit, and gymnastics. In her sixties, she's more fit than most people in their twenties.

The first year is hard.

What to do, as much as what not to do, on the date that marks one year since the start of so much pain, deserves great attention to the heart. Approaching that mark, AnnElise steered her course to Machu Picchu, Peru, with her sister Carol, her daughter Lauren, and other family members.

Intensely interested and prayerfully supportive, we watched for what she would share, knowing it would be completely AnnElise—and completely Sarah.

Then came Facebook photos of handstands, one after another. Maybe they started as a funny pose on this special trip, but what evolved is a story of inspiration.

Sister-daughter-niece handstands in Moray and Lima—and all over Peru—signified the message, helping her fight the sorrow by telling the world about the funny, blissful girl Sarah was. Fighting sadness by sharing happiness.

Back from Peru, her undeniable urge to handstand quickly caught on. It's her upside-down way that helps turn pain into what AnnElise calls "Sharahing Sunshine." What doubled the pleasure was that Carol was part of it from the beginning. Their daily handstand photos became the one thing we most looked forward to.

In the Bennetts' Easter family portrait is AnnElise, handstanding. Against a Southwest Airlines Boeing 737 engine nacelle are AnnElise and Carol, handstanding. Next to the windsock at the Bennetts' grass runway is AnnElise, handstanding.

Carol, a concert cellist, titled one of her photos, "Chilling-With-The-Maestro-Before-The-Concert-Handstand." She did handstands in the orchestra pit and in the dressing room, next to a silver fairy from the ballet *Sleeping Beauty*. To help her sister, she posted a picture of her antics at the door of Homeland Security, and one of her pointing her toes skyward while broken down on the side of the road awaiting a tow truck.

We saw her Sharahing the Sunshine up against a police car (officer in photo, too, smiling), and in front of a ladder truck as the firemen were grocery shopping. When Carol posed with a cat atop her feet, AnnElise replied with a photo of a barnyard banty on the bottoms of her upside-down feet. She titled it, "I'll See Your Cat and Raise You a Rooster Handstand."

Then Carol made a surprising discovery: a photo of Sarah doing a handstand at the beach. When she posted the picture online, the virtual effect was like people rushing to AnnElise and putting their arms around her. Friends and friends of friends reacted with handstand photos in the most unusual places—underwater, in front of the U.S. Capitol Building—and the sunshine spread because these handstands make a statement.

For AnnElise, it's about not letting the sadness win. From the fun comes the deep-seated intent of the act: to Sharah the Sunshine. *Pass it on.*

A Gift

Linda: I had a long but important trip ahead of me. My first fuel stop would be Memphis for lunch with a friend I hadn't seen in nearly thirty years. Then on to Cincinnati to see grandkids.

Myles was ten years old, our oldest grandchild. He was born with Severe Combined Immune Deficiency, commonly known as the "boy in the bubble disease," after the movie with that title. He was born with no functioning immune system, a disease so rare it took a year after his first illness at five months old before getting a diagnosis.

Two previous bone marrow transplants failed, and while preparing for the third try, cancer popped up in the way for the second time. It was lymphoma again. But that's treatable, and only postponed the transplant.

I gathered photos from supportive head-shaving parties held by friends and family around the world. The result was an inspiring YouTube video, "Shaved Heads for Myles," with "Stand by Me" sung by Indiana University's a cappella group, Straight No Chaser. Through the National Marrow Donor Program, we sent thank-you cards and a Superman cape to the anonymous young man in Germany who donated his healthy bone marrow. This hero's gift saved our grandson's life.

My daughter can't be in two places at one time, so our family took turns helping. We either stayed with Myles in the hospital or with his two younger siblings at home while our son-in-law worked. I enjoy both options, but there's something special about staying with Myles. He is known for his teasing and no one is immune, especially doctors and hospital staff. It's one way he combats exhaustion, pain, boredom, and sorrow over friends who didn't make it, as he fights on.

Between treatment interruptions, we did schoolwork and Bible study, built Legos, and watched lots of movies. Over Thanksgiving he chose *Red Tails, Spider-Man,* and *The Avengers*. I think he picked *Red Tails* just for me.

I admire my daughter for the medical warrior she is for Myles, and the great mommy she is to all her children. Changing doctors for the third transplant was a wise choice; Myles was discharged from the hospital several months earlier than expected. While the first one hundred days post-transplant are critical, he did remarkably well, allowing him to be in isolation at home rather than as an inpatient.

Even before discharge, he was given four-hour passes, approvals from his doctor to leave the hospital for short excursions. We used one of those passes the day after Thanksgiving when we went to Lunken Municipal Airport. Little Princess Caroline stayed behind with Mommy, and I took Myles and four-year-old Liam out to the Cheetah and buckled them in for a flight. I explained everything, so they would understand what they were experiencing.

We did several touch-and-goes, staying in the traffic pattern around the airport because Myles couldn't really go anywhere else yet. We looked for his doctor's house in the neighborhoods below and saw the Little Miami and Ohio rivers flowing alongside the airport.

With *Red Tails* fresh on our minds, we scanned the sky for enemy planes. Then turning toward our imaginary prey, we pretended to press a trigger on the yoke, and rolled our Rs as our tongues vibrated the roofs of our mouths: "*BRRRRRAAPTT!*" And I saw him smile. Not just from his lips, but from his whole being beamed this happiness, as his big hazel eyes gazed out the window taking in the newness of the view from aloft.

It thrills my soul to have been with him when he felt well enough to fly, an indescribable gift for which I will always be grateful. And it gave him a unique story to tell when we returned to his hospital room that afternoon.

Preparing his medications, his nurse asked over her shoulder, "How was your pass today? What did you do?"

Ever the jokester, Myles shrugged. "Nothing."

I glared at him in disbelief. "Excuse me?"

His lips barely curled as he tried to restrain a smirk. He held his composure as much to taunt me as to harass the nurse, who turned suddenly from her work. "Oh, sounds like you have something to tell!"

Myles replied offhandedly, like a cool dude, "It was good." Then the grin broke through and he shrugged to maintain the cool: "I went flying with Nanny."

Okie Derby

Mike: The Okie Derby is a precision flying competition, the world's largest proficiency air rally. Created in 1990, the derby generates scholarship funds for flight training. The event is sponsored by the Oklahoma Chapter of the Ninety-Nines, the oldest and largest women's pilot organization with chapters worldwide. The annual exploit offers lots of good-hearted fun with a competitive spirit among participants. For us, getting there was half the adventure, as we avoided thunderstorms along the three-and-a-half-hour flight to Wiley Post Airport.

The derby route became flyable about noon. We took off as participant number seven, rounding the 183-mile, four-leg course in about an hour and twenty minutes. But this was a proficiency rally and scores came from the teams' projections of time and fuel, not from speed.

Contestants were required to estimate their ground speed on the mail-in registration. On the day of the contest, just before an official signals each airplane to start, someone took down our flight-planned fuel burn to the tenth of a gallon. At each airport, there was a different signifier on the ground, a symbol we wrote down as we passed over and went on to the next. This verified we made each checkpoint.

Some folks are great at this. The winners were two seconds and two-tenths of a gallon off. The Oklahoma University team was spot-on their time but a little off on fuel. We overestimated fuel and underestimated ground speed pretty badly; we circled about fourteen minutes in an attempt to cross the line at exactly our forecast time. We came within ten seconds, and I think we would have done better had we remembered where the timing line was.

For all this fun, the reason everyone descended on Wiley Post Airport was to support one deserving person to be awarded a flight training scholarship—one young lady with courage, resilience, and resolve.

Linda: When Leona was a child, she dreamed of flying. Sounds emanating from piston and jet engines flying overhead commanded her attention with a whisper to her soul. Drawn to the awe of flight, the small girl looked longingly to the skies with every passing aircraft. Life events delayed her desire to soar above the earth, but she never let go of her dream.

Removal to foster care while in her teens proved a good thing for Leona. It was a chance to break from her family's history and forge a new path, one of education and career. Not only was she the first in her family to graduate from high school, but to get a bachelor's degree, Leona sometimes juggled two jobs, school, and family.

It was through her church that Leona met Rick and Tim, both deacons, both pilots, and Rick was an instructor as well.

Leona recounted that first meeting. "When I found out Rick was a pilot, I asked a lot of questions, and the conversation finally came around to teaching people to fly. I asked him if anyone can learn to fly, and he said, 'Yes, of course.' I couldn't believe it. I asked, 'You mean you can even teach me?' He laughed as he answered me: 'Yes, even you.'"

When he said that, Leona's heart raced with excitement. Her lifelong dream suddenly felt like a possibility. "I never knew I could fly! Me! Even me! I could actually fly!"

Leona's upbringing didn't allow for that kind of dreaming; it was the self-defeating mindset that taught her to think that those kinds of things are for other people. But now here was Rick, telling her he could help her realize her dream. A door opened and on the other side was wide-open sky and endless possibility.

Mike: By the time we met her, Leona had already flown her first solo cross-country flight, over fifty nautical miles from one airport to another. We were inspired by what we had heard so far. But there was more.

Less than a year before this Okie Derby and scholarship presentation, Rick and Tim were killed in an airplane accident. The tragic loss of her beloved flight instructor and his good friend was a shock to Leona and the community. She had overcome so many setbacks and hardships before, but this one would be tough. Family members questioned her, and she felt the pressure to quit. Should she continue her flight training?

Careful consideration lay worthy between that question and its answer.

With the help and encouragement of other pilots from the Ninety-Nines, the Oklahoma Pilots Association, and the Aircraft Owners and Pilots Association, Leona pulled herself back up by the bootstraps and climbed in the cockpit, to soar again. "I told them it's what I've always wanted to do."

Possibilities

We are at the opening verse, of the opening page, of the chapter of endless possibilities.

—Rudyard Kipling, circa 1921,
upon the future of aircraft, in a letter to
Air Commodore E. M. Maitland

Rocket Man

Linda: While it might have been only natural that Mark Frederick would grow up to be such a highly sought-after airplane builder, he says he never planned it that way. We spent time at the world headquarters of Team Rocket, the company that developed the F1 Rocket, a fast, two-seat experimental airplane. The "F" in F1 stands for Frederick, as in Mark and Cheryl Frederick, who live in Taylor, Texas, on their airstrip they've named Macho Grande.

Mark was born with airplane-shaped genes. His earliest memories are of sitting on his dad's lap in an Aeronca Champ in their Ohio hometown. Two uncles flew in the service, one flying "the Hump" of Burma in the Second World War. By age six, Mark knew nearly every airplane that existed.

As a young adult, Mark moved to Texas for a job in sales, but he had always wanted to build things. So, when the position didn't work out, he went to a cabinet shop to see if they needed help. The boss said if he had a tape measure he could start in the morning. Unfortunately, his ten-foot tape measure wasn't quite what the boss had in mind. When a twenty-five-foot tape was handed to Mark, so were the words, "It's coming out of your paycheck." Fortunately, though, Mark did well. Within six months, he was running a crew and had a company truck.

Mike: The back injury that ended a budding cabinet-making career freed him up to go into aviation full time. His father, a dentist, had always wanted to open a flight school but couldn't find the time. He suggested Mark give it a go and gave him the Champ to start. The students nicknamed the little plane "Raggedy Ann." She served him well at Kittie Hill Flight School in Leander, but in tough economic times the flight training business slowed.

Mark long admired a great-uncle who built a biplane. He also found inspiration in stories of women building airplanes during World War II. Surely, if these people could do it, so could he. With a kit, he would build a small aluminum airplane called a Van's RV-4. Working with aluminum is a lot like working with Formica, and he had worked with miles of Formica in the cabinet business.

One day, Robbie Vajdos, an expert on Stearmans, came to Kittie Hill to pick up an airplane he would ferry to its new owner. He asked Mark if he could buy some fuel for the trip, and that's when he saw Mark's work in progress. Impressed, Robbie referred him to another guy building an RV-4, which led to helping another, and another.

His reputation grew as he guided more people building RV aircraft. Soon, his dedication to perfection and great rapport with customers got him noticed by world record holder Bruce Bohannon. Bruce had secured a sponsor, and he was looking for the right person to build an airplane that would break all records in the "time-to-climb" category. They agreed on a deal and the *Exxon Flyin' Tiger* built by Mark Frederick took Bruce on record-breaking adventures from 1999 to 2006.

Mark also constructed Harmon Rockets for people who bought kits from John Harmon. After building somewhere between eleven and fifteen airplanes, making notes about the process and how to improve it, he realized builders needed an assembly manual. That sparked the idea for Team Rocket. Income from Cheryl's job financed the company. Mark would design and sell airplane kits and provide a manual for his customers who wanted the experience of building their own airplane.

When the manufacturing firm asked how many kits he wanted made, Mark thought he was sticking his neck on the line to say fifty. But forty-eight quick-build F1 Rocket kits sold the first year, and he became known as "Rocket Man."

As the other half of Team Rocket, Cheryl helped unload shipments from the manufacturer and continued to support the company during what Mark called "hiccups." He is quick to credit their partnership. "I could not have done what I did—there would be no Team Rocket without her."

Mark doesn't just build, fly, and teach in airplanes—he races them too. For years, a race called the Sun 100 signaled the start of the world's second largest fly-in, Sun 'n Fun, held each spring in Lakeland, Florida. When he finished building his first RV-4 in 1992, Mark headed to the Sunshine State and entered the race. He enjoyed it so much that in 1996, he hosted a race closer to home. The Texas 100 was a three-turn race in the same format as the Sun 100. But designing it didn't make him immune to navigational errors. He started off in the wrong direction in the race he created!

Mark laughed, remembering, "The first four airplanes off the ground followed me because they figured I knew where I was going. The fifth guy said something on the radio, and then I noticed things I expected to see on the ground were not where they were supposed to be."

He got back on course, and the race was a hit.

Linda: In 2003, Mark tested his skill at the famed National Championship Air Races. The racing over Stead Airport in Reno, Nevada, is a closed-course oval, like a racetrack, as opposed to the various geometric shapes in a cross-country air race. He calls it uncooperative formation flying. "It's the strangest thing to fly formation with guys who don't want to fly formation. They're just trying to beat you. You still have to be predictable, but it's incredibly exciting."

"The Valley of Speed" at Reno is where airplanes that are faster in a straight line do well. Others, like Mark's airplane, are quicker in the turns. Racers use aim points on the ground going into and out of turns because at a high bank angle, the wing may block the pilot's view of a pylon.

Mark got a kick out of one of those aim points. "There was a desk on the ground and some discussion about which side of it to fly on. It turned out we were supposed to fly right over it, then point toward a corner of a fence. The hawk on pylon seven seemed to enjoy watching us whiz by."

He loves the camaraderie and says, "I don't have to be the fastest, but if one of *my* F1 airplanes is, that's just as good."

By 2006, with a fleet of F1 Rockets completed and flying, Mark hosted a gathering at the public airport near his home in Taylor. For sport, he set up another race route and dubbed it the Rocket 100. His promise to declare the winning airplane "Fastest Rocket in the Known Universe" caused excitement among competitive Rocket owners. Canadian Tom Martin won the title. Relaxing in plastic chairs in the hangar after the race, all agreed they should do it again. Now the trophy and title are awarded annually, the race attracting Rocket owners to south Texas each November.

Mike: Meanwhile, one February, the Commemorative Air Force's B-25 *Devil Dog* was stuck in Oshkosh, Wisconsin, with major mechanical problems. Mark flew up to help complete the engine change, then rode with the crew in the vintage bomber back to its home in Georgetown, Texas. Unfortunately, the new engine also had problems. The manufacturer had put limitations on how much oil the engine should burn, and even the new one was consuming too much. Determining the seller had incorrectly installed the engine, Mark argued that the manufacturer's own limitations required the seller to replace it with a new one.

Because of his negotiating skills facilitating the engine exchange, the CAF asked him to join the *Devil Dog* squadron as Chief Maintenance Officer and a pilot. Accepting these positions, he went on the air show circuit. But nobody warned him about the stories he would hear traveling with the B-25.

"I was at Dyess Air Force Base for an air show. It was really hot. I was wiping off oil when over my shoulder I see a tall guy in the distance, coming toward me. I could tell he was on a mission. People walking with a cane don't walk that fast. I watched, thinking he was going to one of the other airplanes on display, but soon it was apparent he was headed straight my way. He reached out and touched *Devil Dog* like it was a tombstone.

"Curious, I invited him to climb inside and said, 'These were pretty awesome airplanes.' I hoped that might open the door to conversation. He replied, 'These blue airplanes saved my life.'

"I thought, wait, no way. This fellow is too young to have served during the war. So, I asked him about it. That's when I learned he and his family had been interred in a detainment camp when he was ten or eleven. He was Filipino. The Japanese built these camps when they occupied many of the islands in the Philippines during World War II. He said his dad would draw a pattern on a piece of paper, hand it to him and send him out with whitewash telling him to paint the rocks just like the pattern."

Mark asked the man if he knew at the time what he was doing. "He said no. He remembers looking up every time B-25s flew over the camp. They were at treetop level—that's how close the enemy was. He could still remember details, like seeing the flaps lower, then the nose come down, then stuff blew up. He said everyone at the camp wanted to cheer but the guards wouldn't let them.

"Years later, he learned what his painted rock symbols meant when a pilot who had flown a B-25 returned and explained that the rocks gave the course, direction, and distance to the targets. Aborigines passed intelligence on the enemy's whereabouts and movement to this man's father and others in the camp. His father then passed the information to him to paint for the pilots."

Then there was the time in Ohio at the 100-year anniversary of the Wright Brothers' first flight, when an elderly man accompanied by his son approached *Devil Dog* with great purpose. Sensing a story might be told, a nearby fellow crew member pulled out a camera and hit record.

The crew from the plane parked next to *Devil Dog* came over to hear what this veteran would say. The man answered questions from crews. He had been on the island of Corsica during the Second World War. He'd flown all variations of the B-25s – the bomber, the one with the cannon, and the "gun nose." The bomber version offered the worst end of the equation – the guys who sat in the nose on that one had a higher mortality rate. They were exposed and vulnerable to enemy fire.

Just then, a World War II re-enactor who had been watching picked up on the invisible. Until that moment, the unspeakable. He asked the man what it was like.

Mark hesitated, trying to retell the story. He reached up anticipating a tear and smudged grease across his cheek. What had caught him off guard that day was the son's reaction – that these stories were new to him. He was hearing his father's story, his fear and his courage, for the first time.

The veteran spoke again. "We flew formation, four, five, or six-ship formation in attack pattern. We attacked the Germans as they were trying to escape through Brenner Pass. We had to blow them up! They had stolen the invention of the proximity fuse and used it against us so they could kill our bombardiers in the front of the plane! To counter that, our formations added another B-25 at the back."

His son was dumbfounded. "He's never told any of us this before!"

The veteran went on to explain. "See, not all the B-25s in the formation carried bombardiers. Only the one flying in the front. But we added another ship to the back with a fully briefed bombardier, so when the B-25 in the front lost their bombardier, the one in the back would fly up to the front of the formation and take over."

Someone on the *Devil Dog* crew pulled out a book of B-25 photos from the war. As the veteran looked over the pictures, the crew members asked him which version of the B-25 he liked best. The one with the gun nose like *Devil Dog* was this gentleman's favorite. The son stood speechless, witnessing his father relive life-changing moments of his youth. Both warbird crews were quiet. Hearing this was a rare opportunity.

The veteran continued. "One time, coming back from a bombing mission, we saw a German flak barge. We landed our bombers and took a large group of gun nose B-25s to kill that barge. The gun nose had biggest bang!" He smiled slightly at the memory of the victory.

The veteran kept talking. "Sometimes we got fighter escorts. The Germans wouldn't shoot at them because our fighters had eight fifty-caliber guns."

He told of more sorties and of his life in the war, and his son repeated himself in awe. "After all these years, he's never told us this!"

That day, another life was changed by a war from long ago.

Linda: Another time, at Oshkosh, again wiping oil off *Devil Dog*, a man walked toward the plane but stopped short about twenty feet away. Mark noticed him and asked, "Wanna see it?"

"No," he replied. "This is as close as I want to get." After a pause, the words tumbled out. "I used to fly these things."

When Mark asked, "How'd that go?" the man shook his head. "It didn't end well. We were shot up bad. I was hit, pilot was hit. The noise was so loud we couldn't hear each other. We hit the water about a mile and a half from the beach. We were in the hospital about nine months. There was an investigation."

His last statement was puzzling.

This was the co-pilot, and he and the other pilot survived but not the rest of the crew. He declined Mark's offer of a ride. The memory was harsh. He walked away. After a few paces, he turned around for one last comment. "I think I feathered the wrong prop."

Mark could only imagine the burden this man must have carried all those years. His heart sank.

Sometimes it's an effort to retell what he's experienced. "When they asked me if I wanted to fly the B-25, I said, 'Ya!' When they said I could fly it in air shows, I was even more excited. 'YA!' But they didn't tell me I would meet these guys. *They* flew the B-25 in anger. They didn't want to go, but they knew they had to. *Theirs* was no air show."

Although he felt unprepared for each of these unique encounters, Mark is grateful. "I met a man who was shot down over the water so many times that the military made him an instructor, teaching how to ditch B-25s."

Mark has this kind of sixth sense about the era, the airplanes, and their pilots. It's more than gratitude, it's like he's one of them. Meeting the few veterans left, empathetic war wounds run soul deep.

While the man with airplane-shaped genes did not plan his life this way, this former cabinet maker has raced through the skies in airplanes he built and, without warning, discovered himself through a B-25.

Life's Disappointments Can't Keep a Good Man Down

Linda: The tumor was benign. That was the good news. It would still need to come out, but Mike Rawls had been through worse. Three stents hadn't kept him down long. Neither had a triple bypass. He would conquer this, too. Although his wife, Pam, and the rest of his family and friends felt the stress each time he was under the knife, they prayed earnestly. Sore from the operation, Mike had time to reflect and to plan, because he didn't plan to stop, only to pause.

That RV-6 kit plane he bought fifteen years prior awaited his mechanical aptitude. Surely the pieces wanted to come together and fly as much as Mike wanted them to. This was his retirement project, a reward for many years of hard work when he finally had both time and money. But his busy life was on hold.

A Cessna Cardinal in his hangar also needed his attention. He had scored a good deal on the damaged plane in an online auction. He decided he would arrange the project in his mind while he recuperated. It wouldn't take him long to fix it once he was able, and he would have something to fly as he built the RV-6.

The memory of acquiring the Cardinal amused him. He had encountered some less confident observers when they saw the mess of a plane as he towed it home. "That airplane on the lowboy got a lot of stares on the way back from Oklahoma. The fuel and hydraulic lines looked like spaghetti, but only if you look at it that way. It will only go back together one way."

Perhaps the doctors who performed his bypass felt that way too, and in that, he would encourage them. This latest surgery could not dampen his will or dim his spark. He had always wanted to fly, and he had never given up.

Mike: No, Mike Rawls had never been a quitter. A yearning for the sky, high energy, and perfectionism were the recipe for motivation when he was a youngster. A stint at his family's restaurant, The San Jacinto Inn, began when he was fourteen, making three dollars and fifty cents a day, "and seven dollars on Sundays. I loved that job."

When he was sixteen, a friend took him to Hobby Airport to get a demo flight in a Cessna. Galvanized, he earned a private pilot certificate by age seventeen. "I planned to get the rest of my pilot ratings in the military and then fly for the airlines. I took survival training and even rode in the back seat of an A-6."

He worked to fund his flight training. His passion for flying, however, couldn't change his height, and the U.S. Marines denied Mike's application for a waiver for acceptance into pilot training. "Military pilots had to be between five-foot-seven and six-foot-three. I'm five-four."

Without sufficient funds for further civilian pilot training, he needed a diversion, a consolation. To help him refocus after this disappointment, his father bought a motorcycle that didn't run so Mike would have something to work on. A week later the motorcycle hummed. Stubbs Cycle in Houston needed a guy like him and by age eighteen, he was their head mechanic. He bought motorcycles, competed in races, and won.

Mike found success, sponsorship, and Pam. Life was fun, but after seven years traveling the racing circuit, it was time to settle down. He went to work for Dow Chemical and stayed for thirty-two years.

"Plant jobs are four on, four off. You can spend money or make it on your time off." This was the impetus for his home-based business, Lawn Mower Clinic, where he worked on over 27,000 pieces of equipment during those same thirty-two years.

While he worked, raised a family, and healed from surgeries, so much time away from flying only deepened his love and strengthened his commitment to return to the air.

Linda: His health restored, he passed an FAA medical exam, free to fly again. This people-loving man began retirement breathing the air of aviation at the Liberty Municipal Airport while waiting for completion of his new hangar home at an air park. He mowed, fixed runway lights, and greeted customers, representing Liberty to visitors landing at the city's front door.

For many years, family, work, and health had demanded his attention and took priority over flying. Mike waited, but he never lost his desire to roam the sky. He wouldn't be an airline pilot, but it all turned out just fine. "General aviation is great. I can go where I want, on my time. I'm like a kid with a new toy."

When the doctor finally cut him loose to fly again, Mike's first jaunt was to the Mustang Beach airport in Port Aransas for a crawfish boil fly-in. These days, when he isn't tinkering with mechanical things, the wheels of his airplane leap skyward as Mike lives out his childhood dreams. That kid can be seen flying his toys in the skies above Southeast Texas and way beyond, to Oshkosh or Sun 'n Fun, or anywhere he pleases, because you can't keep this good man down.

Sign Me Up!

Guest Contributor, Bob Jamison

The final semester for me in college presented an unusual opportunity. No, it wasn't a big paying job, but I had a promotion promised from my high school days as a janitor to a full-grown teller's job. That was quite a step up.

Speaking of stepping up, a neighbor down the hall in the school dormitory showed me a real parachute he had. It seems he borrowed it from his pilot dad. The chute was located in the bucket seat of a war-weary Stearman biplane his dad purchased at some kind of surplus auction sale. Later, that same parachute came in handy.

As luck would have it, the head of the athletic department of the college was a former Air Force pilot instructor. He had collected a few airplanes which he hangared at the Huntsville Airport. One was the famous Piper J-3 Cub; another was a Taylorcraft, while a more advanced airplane was a sleek Globe Swift. Furthermore, he would teach any student to fly and earn his private pilot certificate at a very low cost. I signed up!

The Swift was built like a miniature P-51, I thought, and was almost as beautiful to see it fly. But that airplane was off limits to us "kids," as it was far too fast, and the bottom wing with retractable landing gear was not for the greenhorn beginner.

The first flight was just a ride, I figured. It was the practical approach from the ground school where you learned the airspeed indicator, altimeter, rate of climb (or descent), RPM, needle, ball, and bank (a turn coordinator instrument), and a few other rudimentary instruments, all without an electrical system whatsoever.

The automatic pilot consists of your hand on the throttle, feet on the rudder pedals, and eyes glancing at the instruments and on the horizon. As far as the parachute was concerned, it was the only way to hitchhike a ride to the dorm because the airport was next to the prison. I carried the chute so folks could see I must be a pilot with no car. That would be right.

There were no headphones, so the instructor shouted in your ear and told you how stupid you were for trying to push the throttle past the red line or pulling back the power to approach the stalling speed. The weather was hot, and sweat was pouring down my shirt, and my hands were wringing wet, but I was having a ball even if my pals on the ground could hear the instructor yelling in my ear.

Finally, it was solo time, meaning I had the thing all by myself for the first time. Boy was it quiet, and no hollering. Only the musical sound of the sixty-five-horsepower engine.

Afterward, it was repetitive maneuvers, stalls, coordinated S-turns, and touch-and-goes. What was best was the anticipating of solo cross-country trips with airport stops at prescribed check points.

My instructor, Mr. Joe Kirk, gave me some sound advice before I flew over to Lufkin, Texas, for my flight test. He said, "You are going to mess up, but I think you can pass. Remember this one thing and do not forget it. You keep that ball in the socket!!!" That means watching the turn-and-bank indicator ball that slides to one side or the other if your turn is not perfectly coordinated with stick and rudder. I passed.

Back at the hangar, the check pilot, Mr. A.O. McQueen, was signing my private certificate. A roar was heard, and an airplane barely made it over the roof and did a bouncing landing. We all wondered who that could be. The man flying the plane stopped, made a few circles on the runway and stopped again.

"Get in my pickup, boy. Let's go see what's the matter with that guy."

The pilot was so drunk he couldn't taxi the plane. How he landed it was a point of amazement. We put him in the pickup, and I taxied the plane to the hangar and tied it down.

After the fourth cup of coffee, he said he was an airplane mechanic that did an engine job for the owner, but he couldn't pay for it. So, he signed over the title to the mechanic. I bought it for the price of the bill, which was a bargain, and flew it home the next day after graduation. That is, I owned an airplane before I ever owned a car.

After several glorious flights, a freak storm wrecked the plane while it was tied down. But I already had my eye on a Stearman biplane a farmer bought from one of those surplus auctions but never learned to fly. One of the crop duster pilots had been a Navy fighter pilot in World War II. He told me to buy it and he would teach me to fly the Stearman.

He also gave me a severe warning of its narrow landing gear, its weight, and tricky stall characteristics. He was right. It took me almost as long to solo in that airplane with his help as it did for me to solo in the Cub.

One trip I made in that old Stearman was to Kingsville, Texas. The late Don Shilling was my passenger in the back open cockpit. The airport in Kingsville was huge. It couldn't be the town airport, I thought, so it must be the Navy training base—which it had been. I saw another airport farther west, so I landed there. Here came a jeep with two guys carrying Winchester rifles.

"What are you doing landing here? This is a private airport of the King Ranch!"

I yelled back over the sound of the plane's engine and said, "If you move that jeep over a little, I'll be out of here in one minute," and I was. Flying back home was uneventful until I got to the west edge of Matagorda Bay.

Again, the plane was a military trainer with no electrical system, no radio, no navigation aids, only a compass. Fog and rain were coming in from the Gulf and visibility was limited. I could see the ground now from only 500 feet to remain below the fog and rain. Then the land turned to water. The water turned to blue waves! I'm over the Gulf now, I knew. That perfect maneuver all pilots remember is the 180-degree turn—straight back from where you last saw land. Then I just followed the coast line for a happy landing back home.

What a blast! Looking back over five decades, flying has been a spectacular experience: sometimes challenging, often relaxing, always enjoyable. If I had to do it all over again, I would tell Mr. Kirk, "Sign me up!"

The Road to Nome

Linda: A small camouflage-colored, two-seat, high-wing tailwheel airplane caught my eye as we pulled up to our hangar on a perfect October day. Across the ramp, the pilot rolled up in front of his hangar and shut down. I hadn't seen that plane there before, and I walked over to introduce myself.

As I shook hands with Dave, I peered through the windows and spied camping gear in the rear seat. There was only one place he could have been that weekend: Reklaw, Texas. It's Walker, spelled backward. For real. It's the home of the annual Reklaw Fly-in where about six hundred airplanes descend on a 4,000-foot grass strip. People camp out, fly-bys happen, and aviation camaraderie rules.

Yes, I was sure that was where he'd been, and when he started talking, I could have won "name that accent in one note." It's my favorite—Cajun. The word describes Acadians, descendants of French Canadians who migrated to south Louisiana. Those I have known tend to get excited when telling stories. They have unique whole-body expressions to match their beautiful speech that heavily engages the root of the tongue. I could listen all day to the distinctive flavor of their linguistic gumbo.

Mike: Dave's a welder by trade. His work ethic and skill make him in high demand. One day while cutting pipe, he asked his helper to secure a jack stand to the pipe so he could remove the one he was getting close to as he cut. If they worked it right, adding a third jack stand would allow for removal of the first.

Unfortunately, it wasn't fully secured, and his gloved hand was pinned between the stand and the pipe. Yanking it free with the other hand, he knew he'd need medical attention quickly. The emergency room doctor and nurses examined his mangled hand and sewed it up.

While off work for a few weeks, it was the perfect time for Dave and his wife to take that vacation he had dreamed of for so long—to Nome, Alaska, where they could get away from it all. They drove from their home in New Iberia, through Canada, into Alaska. Dave said when he stopped in Fairbanks at an auto parts store for oil and a filter, he asked the clerk, "Where's da road to Nome?"

Linda: He looked straight at me, perhaps to see if I got it. "Da guy behin-a counta looked at me like I must be da stupidest person in da whole worl. Den he says, 'You got to go by plane. Or, you can wait till da snow come and go by dog sled.'"

According to Dave, the guy behind the counter paused to let the shame sink in. Then he went on, slowly. "There is no road to Nome," he told Dave.

Our new friend shook his head during his reenactment of "There is no road to Nome," his big blue Cajun eyes full of...Cajun.

That was the pivotal moment when Dave said, "Well den, I got to learn how to fly."

Back in Louisiana, at age thirty-nine, Dave did something he had never considered—he earned his private pilot certificate in just three months. With meticulous, thoughtful research, he decided on exactly the plane he wanted and saved his money. Eleven years after driving to Alaska, Dave flew his military-themed Super Cub to "The Last Frontier" and explored its vast beauty for thirty-four days.

A fellow member of SuperCub.org created a web thread for members to follow Dave's journey. Equipped with a GPS tracker reporting his position on the website and cell phones from both the U.S. and Canada, Cajun Dave's adventures quickly drew over ten thousand followers across the globe.

"It was da most amazin ting I learned about da aviation community, dat every single day people would call me and say dey were following my tracker and saw I was headed in their direction, and dey'd invite me to come eat and stay da night at dere house. It was like family everywhere I went!"

An injured hand and no road to Nome led to becoming a member of the family of aviators. I could have watched Dave's Louisiana-style animation and listened to his word emphasis all day. It turns out, we did.

Before Us, They Were

Mike: Our engine hummed smoothly in the still, cool night air. As the distant city's glow became brighter, the calm of our cocoon was rustled when the San Antonio approach controller asked if we could see the airport yet.

No, still looking.

Then, amid sporadically dispersed lights, came a soft white flash; a moment later, a muted green flash—the airport beacon. Yes, we had the airport in sight.

The controller terminated his radar watch over us so we could switch our radio to the airport control tower.

Approaching San Antonio's Stinson Municipal Airport, it was difficult to see the runway lights until we got close. It felt like we were descending into a black hole. The municipal baseball park near the approach end helped illuminate trees near the runway as we coasted in for landing. The gentle bump and the squeak of tires on pavement confirmed we had settled onto terra firma. Stinson's tower controller cleared us to taxi to the terminal where we took a break before continuing our nighttime sojourn.

We love the old stone-faced Art Deco–style terminal. Built in 1936, the building received tender loving care for its seventieth birthday when the city renovated and expanded it while retaining most of the original structure. Old terminals, like old airplanes, need to be spruced up from time to time, but we should never change their timeless souls.

Inside, photographs and memorabilia decorate the halls chronicling Stinson's one-hundred-year past.

Emma Stinson must have been one amazing mom. Not only did she encourage all four of her children to pursue their dreams, she helped out as business manager when they opened a flight school in 1913 in Hot Springs, Arkansas. More agreeable flying weather lured them to San Antonio, Texas, two years later. When the U.S. Army needed more space and moved them out of their first Texas location, the Stinson family leased 500 acres to build a new flying field, today's Stinson Municipal Airport.

Katherine, Eddie, Marjorie, and Jack Stinson made significant contributions to aviation, and the airport named for them is the second-oldest continuously operated airport in the country. Only College Park Airport in Maryland built by the Wright Brothers in 1909 is older.

At Stinson School of Flying, students were beneficiaries of passionate patriotism and piloting. While more is known publicly about Katherine and Eddie, each of the Stinson kids was a dynamic force in shaping aviation.

Katherine

Linda: I wonder if, when Katherine Stinson was growing up in Alabama, anyone outside her family asked her what she wanted to be. Such a question would not have been the norm during her childhood around the turn of the century—1900—because careers for girls were severely limited. Had they asked, she would have told of her plans to study music in Europe and become a piano teacher. A lofty goal, but one within society's expectations.

Her plans would be an expensive endeavor, beyond the family's budget. But something new was on history's horizon. An article about barnstormers and aerial exhibition performers making a thousand dollars a show struck a chord with Katherine. If she flew, she could raise enough for her European music education.

In 1911, most women were grounded. Their "indoor plumbing" qualified them to be homemakers, not pilots. But Katherine's upbringing was not one that fell for gender-related fences and ceilings. After a ride in a hot air balloon, she convinced her parents that flying, and stunt flying in particular, would be the best way to fund her piano training.

Maximilian Theo Liljestrand (Americanized to Max T. Lillie) worked as a pilot for the Wright brothers and was a revered aviator. He also had a flight school in Cicero, Illinois, near Chicago. Katherine asked the Swede to teach her to fly.

Like other flight instructors she asked before him, his response was as swift as a thought: *No.* Petite, young, and female did not describe any aviator Lillie had ever known. Who knows how long "Please" and "No" were exchanged? Katherine was persistent. And she was clever. *How about a ride, then?*

Finally persuaded, he took her up in one of his planes. After four hours of instruction, she soloed. Eight days later, she was the fourth woman to earn a U.S. pilot certificate (July 24, 1912), which she did in a Wright B. Next, she would learn stunt flying.

Even if someone would have asked her what she wanted to be when she grew up, "barnstormer," wouldn't have been in her childhood vocabulary. Twenty-one years old and 101 pounds dripping wet, she became known as the "Flying Schoolgirl," because no one believed she wasn't sixteen.

Katherine had proven to Max Lillie that a woman could fly. Once she won him over, he called her a natural flyer. It is no surprise she is credited with many firsts, any one of which is admirable as a single feat.

Among her records are the first to fly solo at night, as well as records in long-distance flight and airmail services. She was the first precision flyer, and the first known to do pre-flight inspections.

Making history as the first pilot to venture into night sky-writing, she flew over Los Angeles, using flares to spell "CAL." It was 1915, and that summer she and her new Partridge & Keller airplane wowed lucky spectators in Chicago when she became the first woman to perform a loop. And since it wasn't enough to do a simple maneuver, she later added a snap roll at the top of the loop, inventing the "Dippy Twist Loop."

Fans around the world were amazed when she did the kind of maneuvers they'd heard described in the accounts of dogfights over Europe. The first woman to fly in Asia, she was crowned "Air Queen," delighting tens of thousands of spectators in Japan and China.

The few nighttime aerobatic show pilots there are today can thank Katherine for her pioneering work, equipping her plane with magnesium flares fastened to the wingtips. But the loop was her aerial étude of sorts, as she performed this feat around 500 times, with never an accident.

While history thanks Katherine for her tenacity and inspiration, the cost was not insignificant. Flying was expensive. In a classic O. Henry twist, it is said that the family piano was sold to help pay for flight lessons.[29]

The excitement of Katherine's life so inspired the rest of her family that Marjorie, Eddie, and Jack all learned to fly.

I wish I had known Katherine. Her life still touches so many of us. I'm amused that she flew in the New Year's Day Tournament of Roses Parade in Pasadena, California, way back in 1913. While this isn't usually considered one of her many substantial aviation milestones, that made her the first person to pilot a plane in a parade. When I flew over the rodeo parade in Mitchell, South Dakota, not so way back, I thought it was a novelty. I was merely following the legacy of a great pilot.

Through all the barnstorming, record-setting, and mail-toting, Katherine was as much in harmony with her siblings as she was a virtuoso who could set her own tempo. She inspired young girls and gave the boys more to think about than her looks. She was unforgettable to all and arguably the most well-known aviator of her time.

Because of the war, the Stinson School of Flying had to close; the Army needed the space. Although Katherine's attempts to become a combat pilot in World War I were rejected, both Katherine and Marjorie taught men to fly for the military. But Katherine wanted to do more.

---

[29] http://aerofiles.com/bio_s.html and several others

From her strong will to serve, she used her fame on fund-raising tours for the American Red Cross (in its earlier, more earnest days), then went to Europe to drive an ambulance.

As ironically wonderful as her life's piano-to-plane plot twist was, this part of her story arc fell when exposure on the front lines infected her with influenza, then lung-scarring tuberculosis. Her dedication had endangered her health, cutting short a stellar aviation career after only seven years.

But she did so much in those seven years.

When she could no longer fly, she returned to the U.S., settling in Santa Fe, New Mexico, where she met the man she would marry, Miguel Otero, Jr., an airman and later a judge.

Katherine's career changed, too. Far different from early twentieth-century expectations, she became a different kind of homemaker – a much sought-after architect, that is.

Eddie

Mike: Eddie Stinson quit school at age sixteen because he wanted to travel from his home in Mississippi to St. Louis to become a test pilot. That may not have been his answer had someone asked him about career plans, but when he heard about two men building an airplane, he convinced them they needed a pilot – he just didn't mention he wasn't one.

Taking off is optional; landing is not. Eddie didn't do too bad for a kid with no experience. At the farmer's field where he was test flying, his hard landing crunched the airplane. The owners gave it to him as payment. He arranged a deal with the farmer to do chores for room and board and eventually fixed the plane, only to total it on the next landing.

But Eddie wouldn't be deterred. He went to the Wright School in Dayton, Ohio, and learned to fly—*and land.* Soon after, he followed Katherine's lead, flying exhibitions. After gaining some experience, he eagerly shared his passion by teaching others how to master the skills of an aviator. After helping his sisters build the airport in San Antonio, Eddie went to nearby Kelly Field to teach Army Air Corps pilots to fly.

Then a world record-setting endurance flight put him in the limelight. As a result, Stout Engineering, which had bid on a Navy contract, wanted him as their test pilot to fly their new torpedo bomber, the ST-1. He checked it out but didn't like the way the airplane flew and offered ideas to improve it. During a ceremony on the day of acceptance, a Marine pilot stalled and crashed the airplane, and the contract was terminated. That plane was their only prototype. Unfortunately, the engineers had disregarded Eddie's suggestions. Had they listened to him, perhaps this part of history would be a different tale.

Eddie shared Katherine's eye for aircraft design. His fame and experience had given him connections to investors and, when the time was right, he formed Stinson Aircraft Syndicate.

Let's see… 1920s, a "syndicate" in Detroit, not far from Chicago. Perhaps not the best name choice from a public relations, marketing, and sales point of view. Maybe the Stinson group thought so too because a year later, the name changed to Stinson Aircraft Company.

The company produced several successful designs, including a fan favorite, the Stinson Gullwing. Although his very heartbeat covered the beautiful Stinson 108 single-engine airplane, he never saw it off the paper. It was the last airplane the Stinson Aircraft Company built, but Eddie died in a plane crash in 1932, more than a decade before the 108 went into production.

Still, sales benefited from his influence and the family name the airplane bore. Stinson Aircraft's inventory and the type certificate were purchased by Piper Aircraft around 1949. At the time of his death, Eddie was still a world record holder. His 16,000 flight hours made him the most experienced pilot in history at that time.

Marjorie

Linda: Younger sister Marjorie, or "Madge" for short, also learned to fly at the Wright School in Dayton. Like her siblings, she was a natural. When she returned home, she taught students at the Stinson School of Flying in San Antonio, where she earned a reputation as one of the best instructors in the nation.

It has been said that in 1915, Madge was the only woman admitted into the U.S. Aviation Reserve Corps. While our research didn't turn up a "U.S. Aviation Reserve Corps," it could possibly have been the Aviation Section of the Signal Corps, which later became the U.S. Air Force.

Then in 1916, when the Royal Canadian Flying Corps began sending their cadets to the Stinson School for training, they referred to Madge as "The Flying Schoolmarm" and her students as "The Texas Escadrille."

Madge and Eddie trained civilian and Canadian Air Force pilots until World War I began and the facilities were taken over by the government. She is credited with training more than eighty American and Canadian pilots for duty in World War I.

Like her sister, Madge was an exhibition pilot for eleven years and flew airmail routes. Later, she became an aeronautical draftswoman for the U.S. War Department, creating technical drawings for building airplanes and parts.

Where I can relate, however, is in the fact that she was a charter member of the Ninety-Nines, the women's pilot group started by ninety-nine female pilots in the United States. I'm a member of that organization because I appreciate all that women like Madge and Katherine did to open doors for us who came later.

Their flying school helped numerous U.S. and foreign pilots to earn their Aero Club licenses, the precursor to FAA pilot certificates. To honor the accomplishments of these two sisters, in 1997 the National Aviation Club (now part of the National Aeronautic Association) created the Stinson Trophy. The award recognizes a living person for an outstanding and enduring contribution to the role of women in the field of aviation, aeronautics, space, or related sciences.[30]

Marjorie died in 1976, and on July 26 she was cremated, her ashes spread across the Stinson Airfield from a 1931 Curtiss Pusher.

Jack

Mike: By the time we get to Jack, the baby of the family, you might notice a trend. As with baby books, after the first child is born, parents tend to stop counting the first smile, first step,

---

[30] https://naa.aero/awards/awards-and-trophies/stinson-trophy

first tooth lost. We just get busy. Unfortunately, what's left for posterity is but a flash of the person.

The youngest member of the Stinson legacy was Jack, who passed away in May 1976. We know he taught at Stinson School and helped Eddie build Stinson airplanes. We also know he became an aeronautical engineer. Yet we wish we knew the real Jack Stinson, fourth child. He came here before us. Like Marjorie, his ashes were scattered over Stinson Field.

All was quiet that night as we tore ourselves away from this great part of American history. The *Elyminator* beckoned, and as we climbed aboard our sleek steed and headed skyward into the night, we felt the spirit of all those pilots who came before us, right there in that same airspace.

For Further Reading

For Further Reading

1. Ely Air Lines. See http://elyairlines.blogspot.com/.

2. "Who We Are, How We Got Here." See *There I was…flat on my back* by Bob Stevens. Originally published by TAB/Aero, November 1, 1975.

3. "David Rogers – Never Mind the Photos, I've Gone Flying." See *Airplanes, Alligators, and Hi-fin Blues* by J. R. "Bob" Jamison, Tall Tale Publishers, 2001.

4. "Charlie Sisk on Business, Aviation, and Life." See *Selecting and Ordering a Custom Hunting Rifle* by Charlie Sisk and others, 2009.

5. "Small Airports Give Life." See Angel Flight: http://www.angelflight.com/.

6. "Skyway Gypsies." See Charles Collins' website: http://www.charlescollinsgallery.com/.

7. "The Checkered Flag in Kerrville." See *The Origin of the Checker Flag*, by Fred R. Egloff, International Motor Racing Research Center, 2006.

8. "A Fly-In Weekend" and "Jed Keck: A Lucky Guy." See Fort Parker Flying Field: http://www.fortparker.com/ and https://www.historynet.com/noconas-raid-and-cynthia-ann-parkers-recapture.htm.

9. "Hanoi Taxi." See http://www.c141heaven.info/dotcom/aahs/60177_mike_novack.htm.

10. FAA website "Become a Pilot." See https://www.faa.gov/pilots/become/.

11. Aircraft Owners and Pilots Association (AOPA). See https://www.aopa.org/.

12. Experimental Aircraft Association (EAA). See https://www.eaa.org/.

13. Air Race Classic. See https://www.airraceclassic.org/.

14. Sport Air Racing League. See http://sportairrace.org/.

15. Soaring Society of America. See https://www.ssa.org/.

Index

X

Ely Air Lines
Continues in Volume 2

You are cleared direct to Volume 2 of *Ely Air Lines: Select Stories from 10 Years of a Weekly Column.* Squawk the last four of your credit card to get the second half of the series, and enjoy the read!

http://paperairplanepublishing.com

www.ingramcontent.com/pod-product-compliance
Lightning Source LLC
Chambersburg PA
CBHW062016190726
48284CB00012B/287
9781947677029